THE MANY FACES OF VIRTUE

DONALD DEMARCO

EMMAUS ROAD
PUBLISHING

To Fr. Joseph Hattie, O.M.I.,
a man of many virtues and
singular devotion.

THE MANY FACES OF VIRTUE

DONALD DEMARCO

EMMAUS
ROAD
PUBLISHING

© 2000
Emmaus Road Publishing
All rights reserved.

Library of Congress catalog no. 00-106758

Published by
Emmaus Road Publishing
a division of Catholics United for the Faith
827 North Fourth Street
Steubenville, Ohio 43952
(800) 398-5470

Cover design and layout by
Beth Hart

The cover illustration is a detail of Raphael's *The School of Athens*, located in the Vatican Palace. The inserts are details of Michelangelo, Plato, Aristotle, and Pythagoras. Used with permission of Erich Lessing Fine Art Archive and Art Resources, New York.

Published in the United States of America
ISBN 0-9663223-9-8

"The heart itself is but a small vessel, yet dragons are there, and there are also lions; there are poisonous beasts and all the treasures of evil. But there too is God, the angels, the life and the kingdom, the light and the apostles, the heavenly cities and the treasures of grace—all things are there."

Pseudo-Macarius

· CONTENTS ·

III · THE SOCIAL VIRTUES

IV · THE SACRED VIRTUES

· ABBREVIATIONS ·

The Old Testament
Gen./Genesis
Ex./Exodus
Lev./Leviticus
Num./Numbers
Deut./Deuteronomy
Josh./Joshua
Judg./Judges
Ruth/Ruth
1 Sam./1 Samuel
2 Sam./2 Samuel
1 Kings/1 Kings
2 Kings/2 Kings
1 Chron./1 Chronicles
2 Chron./2 Chronicles
Ezra/Ezra
Neh./Nehemiah
Tob./Tobit
Jud./Judith
Esther/Esther
Job/Job
Ps./Psalms
Prov./Proverbs
Eccles./Ecclesiastes
Song/Song of Solomon
Wis./Wisdom
Sir./Sirach (Ecclesiasticus)
Is./Isaiah
Jer./Jeremiah
Lam./Lamentations
Bar./Baruch
Ezek./Ezekiel
Dan./Daniel
Hos./Hosea

Joel/Joel
Amos/Amos
Obad./Obadiah
Jon./Jonah
Mic./Micah
Nahum/Nahum
Hab./Habakkuk
Zeph./Zephaniah
Hag./Haggai
Zech./Zechariah
Mal./Malachi
1 Mac./1 Maccabees
2 Mac./2 Maccabees

The New Testament
Mt./Matthew
Mk./Mark
Lk./Luke
Jn./John
Acts/Acts of the Apostles
Rom./Romans
1 Cor./1 Corinthians
2 Cor./2 Corinthians
Gal./Galatians
Eph./Ephesians
Phil./Philippians
Col./Colossians
1 Thess./1 Thessalonians
2 Thess./2 Thessalonians
1 Tim./1 Timothy
2 Tim./2 Timothy
Tit./Titus
Philem./Philemon

Heb./Hebrews
Jas./James
1 Pet./1 Peter
2 Pet./2 Peter
1 Jn./1 John
2 Jn./2 John
3 Jn./3 John
Jude/Jude
Rev./Revelation (Apocalypse)

Catechism of the Catholic Church

Throughout the text, the *Catechism of the Catholic Church* (United States Catholic Conference–Libreria Editrice Vaticana, 1994, as revised in the 1997 Latin typical edition) will be cited simply as "Catechism."

Acknowledgment

Some of the chapters have appeared, in slightly modified forms, in *Lay Witness*, *Social Justice Review*, and *The Catholic Faith*. The author wishes to thank the editors of these publications for allowing them to reappear in *The Many Faces of Virtue*.

· FOREWORD ·

Not all words are created equal. Some perfectly good ones seem to drag around negative connotations wherever they go. Take prudence, for example. In a self-absorbed culture, what leaps to the mind? *Unhappy prudence.* How about meekness? *Wimpy.* Chastity? *Frigid.* Virtue itself stands in need of a serious public relations overhaul. Vice is daring, hip, and inevitable; virtue is boring, stodgy, and unattainable. Vice wears Armani leather; virtue, a polyester cardigan.

So goes the bias.

The author of this insightful book knows all about it. For over two decades, Dr. Donald DeMarco has been spreading the virtues of virtue before the world's most cynical audience: college students. As a professor of philosophy, a prolific writer, and conference speaker, he has been pointing out what used to be obvious to reasonable people; namely, that goodness, beauty, and truth are knowable, doable, practical concepts. Whether the issue is the imperiled future of parenthood, the power and abuse of language, or the moral implications of biotechnology, the good doctor has kept ahead of the cultural curve.

As kindergarten teachers and Hollywood producers know well, the key to getting your idea across is having a nose for a good story. And DeMarco sports the Cyrano de Bergerac of good story noses. In a world of grunge "mosh pit" enthusiasts, he's a swing dance instructor with a hunch that the soundtrack to the future will sound suspiciously like Benny Goodman.

He may be onto something. Who would have predicted back in the wild and wooly sixties that the dawn of the

new millennium would witness a ballroom dance craze, a
burgeoning chastity movement, and a marked shift toward
traditional mores among many young Americans?

Yes, the Age of Aquarius has reached the age of retirement as the collapse of the sexual revolution has brought
with it the painful discovery that "free love" collects
aggressively on its debts. Seeking escape from the resultant
emotional wasteland, many members of Generation X and
its precocious child, Generation *Why*, have begun to turn
the clock back to the future. Here and there among the
lemmings there is a new sense that there's a cliff ahead,
and you sometimes have to oppose the direction of the
all-knowing herd.

If a movie were made about the author, the high-concept
studio pitch would go, "Socrates meets Garrison Keillor."
And as his latest book proves, the denizens of Lake
Wobegon now have safe passage, by way of a certain hill
outside Jerusalem, to the rarified air of Athens. Goodbye to
the so-called gulf between the scholarly and the popular.
It's just good stuff.

But be warned. The stuff can hook you. Whether you're
a practicing pagan, an observant Jew, an ardent Protestant,
or even a slacker Catholic, you'll see yourself in *The Many
Faces of Virtue*. Or rather, you'll see the self you want to be
and suspect you *can* be. For the thoughtful apologist on the
hunt for sources of unity, you'll find here what every human
person shares in common, the desire to be endlessly happy.

Here everyday heroes become our teachers and we their
eager students. Imagine craving what you thought was cod
liver oil! As DeMarco spins the story behind the story of
the lives of celebrities and ordinary people alike, he lets
their personal virtue shine through without a trace of con-
descension or hagiography. Radio's Paul Harvey, call your

office. Whether it's the day Mahatma Gandhi met Planned Parenthood founder Margaret Sanger, or the secret agony that spurred an athlete on to Olympic gold, or the main fulcrum behind the fall of Communism (hint—it's Polish and rhymes with hope), you'll find yourself hungry for whatever makes these heroes tick.

While the author has already written a book on virtue, this is no sequel. It's fresh good stuff, "ever ancient, ever new." In these delightful true stories, virtue is stripped of any Hallmark card sentimentality or Norman Rockwell fantasy, and reconfigured to engage the reader with the practical means of living life more fully.

Professor DeMarco is a philosopher of culture, which is sort of the opposite of a cable TV pundit. This philosophy combines paradox and practicality, reason and revelation, depth and brevity, gentleness and literary punch. Indeed, the scent of this book will linger in your spirit long after you put it down. While some books on virtue focus on "feeling good about yourself" or "clarifying your values," they often moralize, or else you need a Ph.D. to get through them still awake. But read with even the smallest seed of faith, *The Many Faces of Virtue*—suddenly and without warning—unveils the holy face of Jesus Christ, the supreme model of attractive virtue.

To be honest, the book is probably best enjoyed in solitude—unless you don't mind being caught softly blurting out words like "yes" and "wow." Curl up with this unique collection in your favorite fireplace chair, take it to prayer, or let it charm you on the uptown subway. I hope it gets what it deserves: a huge reading audience.

Patrick Coffin
Los Angeles, California

· PREFACE ·

Love is the source of every real virtue. Every real virtue, then, is an expression of love, a benediction that flows from the human heart, which is the wellspring of love. Because love is the *heart* of virtue, we can easily imagine that the many virtues that proceed from it are its *heartbeats*. One can readily appreciate, for example, that kindheartedness, lightheartedness, and warmheartedness are heartbeats from the heart of virtue. With a little effort, one can further come to appreciate how patience, generosity, forgiveness, chastity, gratitude, and other virtues are heartbeats in the same way.

A writer by the name of Laurence Housman has said, "A saint is one who makes goodness attractive." This is true enough, but it is also true that a good story about good people can make goodness attractive. Given the contemporary mood of cynicism, including the mass media's penchant for making bad news attractive and good news dull, there is a broad and urgent need to help people see the good that lies in goodness. Ordinary, everyday virtues are not only indispensable for holding people, relationships, and society together, but are essential for keeping alive in people's hearts the conviction that goodness is infinitely more exciting, captivating, and rewarding than its opposite. Vice, when all is said and done, is a banality, a failure of the moral imagination.

The following forty-eight heartbeats not only commend and clarify a goodly number of virtues, but give them an existential appeal by explaining many of them in the context of inspirational stories. I have divided the heartbeats into four groups—the personal, the interpersonal, the social, and the sacred—in order to emphasize how, though distinct, they nonetheless build on each other to form a comprehensive view of life. The moral life is organic. Virtues need each other in order to assemble that most prized, though often under-appreciated human treasure: *moral character*. And without moral character, society is in peril.

Donald DeMarco
Kitchener, Ontario

· I ·

THE PERSONAL VIRTUES

· DOCILITY ·

The words "doctor," "doctrine," and "docility" are etymologically connected. Their distinct meanings all converge upon the same reality. This point is illustrated, for example, when we say that a doctor teaches a doctrine to students who are docile. A doctor is primarily a teacher. A doctrine is that which he teaches. Docility is the virtue of teachableness in students who allow themselves to be taught by a doctor, who teaches them a doctrine.

Docility, according to Saint Thomas Aquinas, is related to the virtue of prudence.[1] Specifically, it is that part of prudence that allows us to acquire knowledge through the teaching of another. The Angelic Doctor points out that even the most learned people need to be docile, since no man is completely self-sufficient in matters of prudence. We all stand in great need of being taught by others.

Intellectual Blindness

It is easy for people to be docile when they are aware of their own desperation. If one is lost in a foreign city, let us say, it is easy to be docile to a local citizen who can give us directions. The great problem with docility, however, is that people are often unaware of their own desperation. That is, they do not know they are lost.

---

[1] *Summa Theologiae*, IIa IIae, q. 49, art. 3.

Contemporary university students, as Allan Bloom has pointed out in *The Closing of the American Mind*, are notoriously lost and indocile. When a person who is lost is also indocile, needless to say, his indocility assures that he will continue to be lost.

Aquinas teaches that there are two obstacles in particular that lie in the path of acquiring the virtue of docility. One is laziness, the other is pride. Pride, however, is far more insidious than laziness. The lazy person has difficulty concealing his laziness, even from himself. Perhaps part of the reason is that he is even too lazy to think up ingenious excuses! The lazy person usually knows that he is lazy. Therefore, he recognizes his laziness as a vice, not a virtue.

But the proud person, who often has contempt for those who know things that he does not know, is not only able to conceal his indocility (as well as his pride) from himself, but is able to misinterpret his vice as a virtue. Thus, the indocile person who is proud may think that, by his stubborn refusal to allow others to "impose" their ideas on him, he is maintaining an open mind.

Mind Without Matter

We now come to what may be the single greatest problem concerning docility: a false conception of an open mind. The mind that is forever open, forever fearful of losing its freedom, forever indocile to truth, is entirely useless. Such a mind is really indistinguishable from no mind at all.

Samuel Butler, the nineteenth-century British novelist, saw through the hoax of the eternally open mind when he wrote:

> An open mind is all very well in its way, but it ought not to be so open that there is no keeping anything in or out

of it. It should be capable of shutting its doors sometimes, or it may be found a little draughty.

G.K. Chesterton agreed. He, too, thought that the mind has a nobler function than serving as an intellectual breeze-way between the ears. The mind, when it functions properly, seizes, apprehends, and grasps its object. In criticizing the notion of the ever-open and never-closed mind, as espoused by H.G. Wells, Chesterton stated:

I think he thought that the object of opening the mind is simply opening the mind. Whereas I am incurably convinced that the object of opening the mind, as of opening the mouth, is to shut it again on something solid.

Students and others who are indocile because they distrust or despise their teacher, or because they fear the truth or the personal responsibilities that knowledge brings, are not preserving their independence, but squandering their intellects. They are like the ultra-fastidious person who, in waiting for the perfect friend to come along, never meets anyone he deems good enough to be his friend and, as a result, suffers atrophy of the heart.

Nothing to Stand on

One of the curious features concerning the triad of doctor, doctrine, and docility is that it is now quite popular to prize the position of doctor, but to despise both doctrine and docility. But the status of doctor that so many people esteem is hollow and wholly unworthy of their admiration. If a doctor has no doctrine to teach (Who knows what truth is?) and no docile students whom he can teach (because they fear ideas that are "imposed" on them), then his role is entirely bankrupt and useless. He is the equivalent of the buggy-whip salesman who has neither producers nor consumers.

The mark of the docile person is his willingness to be taught. But since docility is part of prudence—the virtue of realism—the only thing the docile person wants to know is the truth. The roots of docility are in humility and self-knowledge, while its fruits are in realism and practicality.

In a series of reflections on the Trinity entitled *Celebrate 2000!*, Pope John Paul II reminds his flock of the eminent role of Christ the Teacher, who reveals God to man and man to himself. He proclaims:

> The majesty of Christ the Teacher and the unique consistency and persuasiveness of His teaching ... can only be explained by the fact that His words, His parables, and His arguments are never separable from His life and His very being.[2]

The Christian should have no misgivings about being docile to Christ the Teacher or the teaching ministry of Holy Mother Church. It is sad to witness so much indocility both to Christ and His Church by Christians who fall prey to the distortions of truth promulgated by our secular world.

Pope John Paul II has reminded us again of the importance of docility amidst the wiles of the world in his apostolic letter *Tertio Millennio Adveniente*. There he quotes Vatican II's *Declaration on Religious Liberty*: "The truth cannot impose itself except by virtue of its own truth, as it wins over the mind with both gentleness and power."[3]

---

[2] Pope John Paul II, *Celebrate 2000!* (Ann Arbor, MI: Servant Publications, 1996), 27.

[3] *Dignitatis Humanae*, no. 35, as translated in Austin Flannery, O.P., ed., *Vatican II: The Conciliar and Post Conciliar Documents* (Northport, NY: Costello Publishing Co., 1975).

· MEEKNESS ·

My electric typewriter has a built-in dictionary of 60,000 words. Whenever my typing of any of these words is incorrect, an electronic bell is activated, gently alerting me to the fact that I have made a spelling error.

My "spell check," however, is given to producing many false alarms. I can get by very quietly with "jejune," "heuristic," and "obloquy." But when I enter the word "meekness," the automatic beep sternly calls me to task. Being a philosopher of culture, however, and confident that I can properly spell "meekness," it is my mental bell that I am more attuned to, and that more spiritual alarm reminds me that not only the word "meekness" but its very meaning is conspicuously absent from popular discourse. For many, it is simply assumed that "meekness is weakness," and surely not a virtue.

Keeping Our Grip

The irony is that meekness, indeed a virtue, is the one virtue above all that allows us to remain ourselves in the midst of adversity. It allows us to maintain self-possession when adversity strikes, rather than be possessed by the adversity itself.

Meekness is more synonymous with empowerment than it is with weakness because, as Saint Thomas Aquinas wrote, meekness makes a man self-possessed.[1] Dionysius said

---

[1] *Summa Theologiae*, IIa IIae, q. 157, art. 4.

that Moses, surely no Milquetoast, "was deemed worthy of the divine apparition on account of his great meekness." According to Saint Hilary, "Christ dwells in us by our meekness of soul." When we are overcome by anger, we lose the sense of ourselves that allows God to dwell within us. Anger excludes God; meekness invites His presence.

Since meekness is self-possession in the face of adversity, it enables a person to do good in response to evil. Meekness is not cowardliness, timidity, or servility; it is the power that restrains the onslaught of anger and subjects it to the order of reason. While it may be more natural to express anger when one is assaulted, meekness is the higher path. It prevents evil from completely overcoming the person who is already suffering enough from evil. Meekness prevents this suffering from advancing to the precincts of the soul—first to depression and then to despair.

All the Rage

People speak approvingly of someone "going ballistic" in the face of even a slight offense. "Feminist rage" is presumably justified on the basis of the acceptability of revenge for perceived injustices. But the unleashing of wrath is not the self-possession that Saint Thomas had in mind. The anger that leads to revenge can be futile, if not counterproductive. As Saint Bonaventure warned, becoming upset and impatient over the failings of someone is like responding to his falling into a ditch by throwing oneself into another. If the desire for vengeance is not restrained, the administration of justice becomes merely a repayment of evil with another evil. And retaliation of this kind has a tendency to escalate conflict, with each blow being repaid with yet another.

Courage, Not Prozac

Real-life stories are often the best means of illustrating a virtue. On a June morning in 1993, David Gelernter, a Yale University computer scientist, opened what he thought was an unsolicited doctoral dissertation. The package exploded in his hands, nearly blowing off his right hand and severely damaging his eyesight, hearing, and chest. Gelernter had joined the list of casualties of the "Unabomber," Theodore Kaczynski.

If anyone had a right to see himself as a victim, one might say, it is David Gelernter. But he will not wear that badge, and he will not invite the outpouring of public sympathy that goes with it. Nor does he want to be seen as a survivor. He does not want to be relegated to categories that are suspiciously "politically correct." He wants to be known as a human being, a husband, and a father. We know a great deal about David Gelernter and his struggles with adversity, assault, and affliction, because he has written eloquently and insightfully about it in his book, *Drawing Life: Surviving the Unabomber*.

There were times when he could be discouraged, but at no point was he depressed. Depression, he writes, "is a pathological state." On the other hand, "discouragement is a moral state, a failure of the heart; you treat it by taking courage, not Prozac."[2]

Victims of Anger

A person in adversity wants to be able to act, not acted upon. It is so easy to be consumed by anger. But that is a way of being acted upon, even though the anger flows

---

[2] David Gelernter, *Drawing Life: Surviving the Unabomber* (New York: Free Press, 1997), 86.

directly from one's own wounds. Hence, Gelernter stead-
fastly eschews the label "victim." A person who readily
accepts the tag of "victim" is already engaging, if not floun-
dering, in self-pity. "When you encourage a man to see
himself as a victim of *anything*—crime, poverty, bigotry, bad
luck—you are piling bricks on his chest."[3] Self-pity, the
failure to summon the positive power of meekness, is like
piling bricks on your chest. Your best friends are the ones
who help you heave them off.

Lady Diana Cooper, who was rather well-off, had trouble
finding the meekness to deal with the unavoidable facts of
human existence, let alone the devastation wrought by
the Unabomber. "I do not think," she once exclaimed,
"servants should be ill. We have quite enough illness ourselves without their adding to the symptoms." How many
of us, who complain about the most trivial inconve-
niences, fail to forestall our anger by exercising a bit of
meekness? A hockey player who earns approximately ten
million dollars a year demands to be traded to a larger city
so that he can go shopping without being badgered by
adoring fans. An irate teenager leaves home because her
mother requires her to take out the garbage. A distraught
motorist flies into a violent rage because he is once again
stuck in traffic.

David Gelernter's memoir reveals the soul of a politically
incorrect moral hero. In an age when "victimology" is
temptingly trendy, and "conspicuous compassion" has
replaced "conspicuous consumption" as a natural pastime,
it is reassuring that there are still moving examples of men
who have the meekness to remain self-possessed when
nearly everyone around them is advising them otherwise.

---

[3] *Ibid.*, 46.

· REVERENCE ·

A plane carrying the Cincinnati Reds baseball team flew into severe turbulence. One of its passengers, the irrepressible Pete Rose, turned to a teammate and said: "We're going down. We're going down and I have a .300 lifetime average to take with me. Do you?" His teammate's response is unrecorded.

Pete Rose may get into heaven, but it will not be on the basis of his career batting average or the fact that he surpassed Ty Cobb in total lifetime hits. Rose's present tragedy is that, despite his impressive baseball accomplishments, he is barred from Cooperstown's Hall of Fame. "I was raised," Rose once confessed, "but I never grew up." When his autobiography was published, the ecstatic author exclaimed that it was the best book he had ever read. He quickly qualified the praise he seemingly conferred upon his own handiwork by pointing out that *Pete Rose: My Story*, which he "co-wrote" with Roger Kahn, was the only book he had ever read.

Striking Out

Another man from the world of baseball, umpire Tom Gorman, was far less accomplished on the baseball field than Pete Rose. He faced the hereafter with stoic suspense. When he passed away in 1986, he was buried in his umpire's uniform. Placed in his hand was a ball-and-strike indicator. The count read three balls and two strikes.

Baseball, like anything else, can be absorbing to the point that nothing else matters. G.K. Chesterton once remarked that the difference between the poet and the lunatic is that the former is content to get his head inside of heaven, while the latter wants to get all of heaven inside of his head.

Who's Number One?

People are self-absorbed or outgoing, poetic or lunatic, saintly or devilish. The main difference between these two groups is the presence or absence of the virtue of reverence. The ruling attitude of the reverent person is that there is something more important, more beautiful, more wondrous in the universe than himself.

Reverence, in this sense, is indispensable for religion. "The soul of the Christian religion is reverence," wrote Goethe. The opening sentences of Saint Augustine's *Confessions* offer us an excellent example of the reverent man who is emerging from his cocoon of self-absorption, folly, and sinfulness:

> Great art Thou, O Lord, and greatly to be praised; great is Thy power, and of Thy wisdom there is no end. And man, being a part of Thy creation, desires to praise Thee,—man, who bears about with him his mortality, the witness of his sin . . . for Thou hast formed us for Thyself, and our hearts are restless till they find rest in Thee.

Reverence and humility are kindred virtues. The humble man, because he is not inflated by his own accomplishments, possesses a certain realism that disposes him to have reverence for the things of God. Humility flows from a realistic appraisal of self; reverence flows from a realistic appraisal of God and His creation. If one is not humble, he is not likely to be reverent.

Cosmetic Fixation

The secular world finds virtue in irreverence—it's commonly viewed as proof of one's independence—largely because it does not find humility particularly attractive. "The real drawback to marriage," Oscar Wilde has acidly opined, "is that it makes one unselfish. Unselfish people are colorless." The pressure to be "colorful" has been a boon to the cosmetic industry. Vanna White, whose most notable accomplishment in life is turning letters for TV's "Wheel of Fortune," would seem to be an unlikely candidate for being solicited to offer us sound, philosophical advice. Nonetheless, when asked about her philosophy of life, she urged her public to: "Be happy. Stay healthy. Feel good. Stay in shape. Treat others like you want them to treat you. Keep moisturizer on your face." Media advice is usually thin on humility and scant on reverence, but predictably rich in appearance and luxurious in trendiness.

Our secular world holds the virtue of "open-mindedness" in high esteem. But this may be spoken more from the lips than from the heart. An excessive preoccupation with such small and stifling enterprises as batting averages and face moisturizer does not make for an expansive life. Reverence, on the other hand, not only opens our minds, it also opens our hearts. By uniting us with the cosmos, it enlarges our life and opens it to innumerable enjoyments and satisfactions.

Wonderful Vision

Helen Keller was once asked, "Is there anything worse than not having sight?" "Oh yes," she hastened to explain, "it would be much worse to have your sight but not have vision." Reverence is the virtue that allows us to have vision. There are things that are more important than our ego. Reverence gives us the vision to see what they are and, in the spirit of Saint Augustine, the heart to find peace in what they convey.

"The world will never starve for want of wonders," wrote G.K. Chesterton, "but only for want of wonder." The reverent person will never run out of wondrous experiences, because he is in tune with the cosmos. But the irreverent person, who lacks the cultivated capacity to appreciate how wondrous the world really is, will find life empty. His lack of reverence will, in effect, banish all wonder from his life.[1]

---

[1] Donald DeMarco, *Heart of Virtue* (San Francisco: Ignatius Press, 1996), 203.

· CHASTITY ·

Sigmund Freud believed that the sexual appetite, which he referred to as the "id," was always at odds with the voice of reason, which he termed the "super-ego." Given this radical conflict, this irremediable antagonism between the demands of instinct and the claims of reason, life, for Freud, was cursed with unredeemable dissatisfaction. Though he did not understand chastity and had no place for it in his psychology, Freud did understand that without chastity, man is doomed to a life of hopeless discontent.

May I Have This Dance?

Chastity, which in the Russian tradition is called "the wisdom of wholeness" (*tselomudrie*), is the virtue that brings the sexual appetite into harmony with reason. Sex and reason are no more in conflict with each other than dancing and music. Chastity, however, like any other virtue, requires a certain amount of effort and practice before it becomes a virtuous habit. One can dance, but one must adapt it to the right music. It is foolish to condemn dancing as a result of one's frustrations in trying to march to a waltz. The siren songs of prurient commercial advertising, for example, are not fit accompaniment for human sexuality.

Chastity, therefore, does not require the renunciation of sexuality, but the right use of it. There are times when human beings should abstain from sexual pleasure, but it is not necessary to abstain from activities that are conducted in accord with reason. By reason, we are referring not to an abstract and impersonal set of rules separated from life, but the capacity to be realistic. Reason is a light that illuminates what we are doing so that we can behave in a way that is consistent with our best interest.

One of the fundamental problems that unchastity brings about is a blindness that leads directly to acts of imprudence. A person who is inflamed by lustful desires is hardly in a position to do what is good for himself or anyone else. It is well-known that prostitutes can operate very effectively as spies by first seducing their targets and then educing from them the valuable information they possess. The intemperate military leader of the Old Testament, Holofernes, lost his head both figuratively and literally because of his lust for Judith: "Her sandal ravished his eyes, her beauty captivated his mind, and the sword severed his neck" (Jud. 16:9).

Unbrotherly Love

Unchastity can be the ruin of a personality. In Shakespeare's *Measure for Measure*, Angelo offers to spare the life of Isabella's brother, Claudio, who faces death because of sexual misconduct, if she consents to sleep with him. When Isabella, who is a novice in a cloistered order of nuns, discusses the matter with her brother, she is horrified to discover what a despicable rake he has become as a result of his carnal misadventures.

"Death is a fearful thing," says Claudio, who has little regard for his sister's chastity. "And shamed life is a hateful [thing]," replies Isabella. Claudio becomes more earnest in his plea: "Sweet sister, let me live: What sin you do to save a brother's life, nature dispenses with the deed so far it becomes a virtue." Her response is most emphatic:

> O you beast! O faithless coward! O dishonest wretch! Wilt thou be made a man out of my vice? Is't not a kind of incest, to take life from thine own sister's shame?

She breaks off any further discussion by exclaiming that, for Claudio, fornication was not a lapse but a lifestyle: "Thy sin's not accidental, but a trade, mercy to thee would prove a bawd: 'Tis best that thou diest quickly." Claudio's preoccupation with sexual pleasure, which had become a "trade," or a cold-blooded way of life, poisoned his soul to the degree that his own sister's honor meant nothing to him. In fact, poor Claudio had lost all sense of right and wrong. He loved his own life inordinately and to the exclusion of all else. Lust had taken possession of him.

Surrounded by Sin

Chastity is a most honorable virtue. It honors the self as well as the other. It may be a difficult virtue to attain. Yet the greater part of its difficulty lies not so much in the intensity of sexual desire itself, but in the fact that sexual desire is constantly being aroused by a social environment that can think of little else.

Friedrich Nietzsche, no friend of Christianity, recognizes the validity of this point. In *Thus Spake Zarathustra*, he begins his chapter "Of Chastity" by stating, "I love the forest. It is bad to live in towns: too many of the lustful live there." Saint Thomas Aquinas, long before the days of mass media, understood too well the dangerous role environmental seduction could play:

There is not much sinning because of natural desires . . .
But the stimuli of desire which man's cunning has devised
are something else, and for the sake of these sins one sins
very much.[1]

Modern man alleges that "chaste is waste" and "virtue
can hurt you." But the contemporary fascination with parts
is itself a waste and a source of harm, for it enfeebles the
whole. Chastity is, indeed, the virtue of wholeness, the
virtue that prevents us from the disgrace of being reduced to
a mere appetite (cf. Catechism, no. 2339). The gratification
of appetite may bring about pleasure, but it cannot bring
about joy, which is the experience of the whole person.

The chaste person does not sacrifice joy for pleasure.
Rather, he integrates pleasure with joy so that he has both
and is thereby a more complete human being. Moreover,
because the heart of chastity is love, the chaste person is
more faithful to those whom he loves and therefore refrains
from making the other person subordinate to his pleasure.
Chastity frees us to love others justly and faithfully.

---

[1] *Summa Theologiae*, IIa IIae, q. 142, art. 2.

· PATIENCE ·

We are not a patient age. Since the time Ogden Nash penned the witticism, "Candy is dandy, but liquor is quicker," the pace of life has become even more hectic. We are in love with speed. We want "fast food," "instant replay," immediate seating," "instamatic cameras," "rapid recoveries," and "quick fixes."

We want to spend money before we have time to acquire it, and arrange for our children's college education before we have them baptized. We can dine in Paris, catch the Concorde, and have indigestion in New York. A certain Sean Shannon has become a kind of theatrical icon in our frantic age by reciting Hamlet's "To be or not to be" soliloquy at the breakneck speed of twenty-four seconds. A best-selling book is entitled *If It Works, Break It*. Things become obsolete the moment they are purchased. In the world of computer engineering there is the saying, "If it travels at the speed of light, it is too slow." Perhaps Goethe's character Faust provided the slogan for the modern age when he exclaimed, "And cursed, above all, be patience."

The old adage, "Patience is a virtue, possess it if you can; seldom in a woman, but never in a man," is no longer as cynical as it once seemed, since we no longer prize patience as a virtue. "Why wait?" people ask, and then do not bother to wait for an answer. People have trouble waiting for the traffic light to change, let alone waiting for their coffee, waiting before they jump to conclusions, or waiting until marriage.

Not So Fast

If speed is a way of life for our restless age, then "speed kills" is its epitaph. The paradox is that speed does not intensify or improve our experience of life. Rather, it destroys it. By contrast, patience gives us the opportunity to practice discernment, to test what is true, and separate it from what is not true. Patience allows us to live more fully and realistically.

The New Testament makes it clear that God is patient with man, and that man must be patient in order to receive God's Word and allow it to bear fruit. As Our Lord Himself says, the seeds that fall in good soil "are those who, hearing the word, hold it fast in an honest and good heart, and bring forth fruit with patience" (Lk. 8:15).

Saint Thomas Aquinas teaches that patience is a part of fortitude.[1] Unlike fortitude, however, which remains steadfast when there is danger of death, the most difficult thing to endure, patience consists in holding fast to what is good in the midst of sorrow or pain. He is in fundamental agreement with Saint Augustine, who states that through patience a person is able to bear an evil without being disturbed by sorrow, so that he does not abandon those goods that might advance him to better things.

If we allow ourselves to be enlightened by the Christian tradition, then the present obsession with speed, an unambiguous symptom of impatience, is the immediate result of trying to avoid sorrow. But what is the sorrow or pain that modern man is trying to escape? It is the sorrow that results when one does not believe that his life is good. This absence of good, in itself, is reason enough for sorrow.

---

[1] *Summa Theologiae*, IIa IIae, q. 136, art. 4.

"It is sad not to see any good in goodness," laments the Russian novelist Nikolai Gogol. This is a most insightful comment on modern man, who has lost a sense of the goodness of life. Unable to tolerate his boring situation, he reaches out frantically for some form of excitement, distraction, or stimulation that will make him forget the pain of his emptiness.

Hold Fast to What Is Good
(1 Thessalonians 5:21)

We need patience to endure the sorrow that besets us so that we do not betray the good we have. This is the thinking of Augustine and Aquinas. But if we have lost our sense of the good, our problem cuts deeper than a mere absence of patience. We must first learn to discern what is good and hold on to it with love. Then patience in times of sorrow will help us to be faithful to that love. We are an impatient society, to be sure, but we are a society that has lost its sense that what it has is good and worth suffering for.

Malcolm Muggeridge, in an interview with a Russian writer by the name of Anatoli Kusnyetsov, asked him how he managed, during Stalin's reign of terror, to maintain his Christian orientation. Kuznetsov answered for himself and many other Russians. He said that was because Stalin made one fatal error: He neglected to suppress the works of Count Leo Tolstoy.

Tolstoy's writings were celebrations of the good of Christianity. These classics educated, even inspired, his readers to see that it was far better to suffer great wrongs than to abandon their Christian faith. They taught the nobility of patience and, as a result, his readers practiced it.

Patience, as Aquinas writes, is not the greatest of all virtues. It is a virtue for those who have found something good enough to suffer for. But for those whose boring lives drive them to desperation, what they most need is not patience but someone to love.

· DETERMINATION ·

Popular interest in the Olympic games involves a curious irony. Despite our culture's unswerving commitment to a life of comfort and convenience, people are drawn to the Olympic spectacle precisely because it celebrates the place of discomfort and inconvenience. Wealth without work, marriage without sacrifice, and sex without tears are bogus ideals. People really want to know how to surmount difficulty, not how to avoid it.

The great Olympic stories, the ones that survive and continue to be a source of hope, are the ones that tell about the human journey from hardship to victory. The motion picture *Chariots of Fire* tells of the Scottish runner, Eric Liddle, who refused to run on Sunday because of a religious objection. Liddle, with the cooperation of a Jewish athlete, traded his best event, the 100-meter, for the 400-meter, in order to avoid running on the Lord's Day. Despite taking on the added hardship of running in an event he had not trained for, Liddle streaked to victory and won a gold medal for his country.

In a previous Olympiad in London in 1908, an American student by the name of Foster Smithson protested his having to run the 110-meter hurdles on Sunday by running with a Bible in his hand. He not only won the race but set a world record in the process.

Painful Hurdles

Canada's Anne Ottenbrite nearly didn't compete in the 1984 Olympiad in Los Angeles. She missed the Canadian Olympic trials that year when she suffered a dislocated right kneecap. Nonetheless, Canadian officials decided to put her on the swimming team. Then, on arriving in Los Angeles, she suffered whiplash as a passenger in a car accident. Yet she swam to win gold, silver, and bronze medals.

Perhaps the greatest long-distance runner of all time is Finland's Paavo Nurmi. Nurmi knew all about hardship: He grew up in a one-room dwelling with four siblings and his widowed mother, who earned a meager wage as a laundress. When he was young, he practiced by running behind trolley cars. At the 1924 Paris Olympiad, he won five gold medals in long-distance events over a span of just four days. He won the 1,500-meter and fifty-five minutes later entered and won the 5,000-meter, setting new Olympic records in both events.

Ray Ewry was the victim of an unknown disease during his childhood. He was confined to a wheelchair and doctors predicted that he would never walk. Some even predicted an early death. Nonetheless, Ewry began to perform therapeutic exercises to strengthen his legs. He ultimately developed the ability to make powerful leaps from a standing position. At age twenty-seven, he entered the first modern Olympiad in 1896 in Athens and won all three standing-jump events. He duplicated this feat in Paris in 1900. He won two more championships: Athens in 1906 and London in 1908, at the age of thirty-five. In all, he entered ten Olympic events and won all ten, an accomplishment that remains unequalled.

Bob Mathias was diagnosed at eight years of age as having pernicious anemia. His doctor required him to take daily afternoon naps and forbade him from participating in sports for five years. At seventeen, he won the grueling decathlon at the 1948 games in London, thereby becoming the youngest athlete ever to win a gold medal in track and field. Mathias won the decathlon again in Helsinki four years later.

No Defeat in Disability

The Hungarian Karoly Takacs suffered the loss of his right arm in a grenade explosion in 1939. Through intense training, he learned to shoot with his left hand and won gold medals in rapid-fire pistol shooting in the Olympic games of 1948 and 1952.

Walter Davis was stricken with polio when he was eight. Although he recovered a few years later, the disease had left his legs weak, necessitating a strict regimen of leg exercises. Nonetheless, he won a gold medal at the Helsinki games in 1952, jumping three-fourths of an inch over his 6'8" height.

An illness during infancy left Harold Connolly with a withered arm that was four inches shorter than his other arm. In addition, he had broken the arm four or five times in football games. He took up the hammer-throw as a student at Boston College in order to strengthen his arm. In 1956 he set a new Olympic record in that event.

The parents of Rafer Johnson and their five children lived, for a time, in an abandoned railway car. When he was twelve, Rafer's leg was badly mangled in a machinery accident and required surgery. Johnson went on to win the decathlon in the 1960 Rome Olympiad. He later became the director of the Kennedy Foundation, and was chosen to light the torch at the 1984 Olympic games.

Wilma Rudolph was the seventeenth of nineteen children born to poor parents in Tennessee. Severe pneumonia and scarlet fever at age four made one of her legs useless. For more than two years, she was confined either to a wheelchair or to bed. Her brothers and sisters took turns massaging her legs. As a result of their unremitting care, she was able to walk with special shoes by the time she was six. Ten years later she won a bronze medal at the Melbourne Olympics. At the following Olympiad she won three gold medals.

The best stories, that is, the ones from which we draw inspiration to live by, are not those of people who win huge sums of money in a lottery and then retire to become couch potatoes (Mad Couch Disease). They are the stories of people who overcome hardships through sheer determination to accomplish great things. They are stories that supply us with real hope. Perhaps our greatest disability is an absence of determination.

· TEMPERANCE ·

In January 1936, a meeting took place between Mohandas Gandhi and Margaret Sanger. The subject of their conversation on that auspicious occasion was contraception. Mrs. Sanger was, at that time, the high priestess of the birth control movement. For her, as well as for her legion of followers, "birth control" meant *contraception*. Gandhi had a different understanding of birth control. For him it meant temperance, or *self-control*.

During their meeting, Sanger tried to convince Gandhi of the moral legitimacy of contraception. She wanted people to rely on contraceptive technology. Gandhi, who regarded the use of contraception as sinful, wanted people to rely on human virtue. He offered, therefore, a more human and less technological remedy for avoiding unwanted pregnancies. The great Hindu leader proposed a method in which the married couple would abstain from sexual union during the wife's fertile period.[1]

On Opposite Sides of the World

It may be that no two more utterly disparate world figures of the twentieth century ever met to discuss a moral issue of such critical and global significance. Sanger was a libertine whose religion was pleasure. In a letter to her sixteen-year-old granddaughter, she advised that "for intercourse, I'd say

---

[1] *The Works of Gandhi*, vol. 4, 45-48.

three times a day was about right." Gandhi, known as
Mahatma or "Great Soul," was an ascetic who dedicated his
life completely to truth and peace. He led his people in
India to their political independence, and both his example
and his philosophy have continued to inspire others who
labor for the same goals, including Reverend Martin Luther
King and his fight for civil rights.

It is not an exaggeration to compare this meeting
between the voluptuary and the ascetic with that between
Satan and Christ after the latter had fasted for forty days
in the desert. Margaret Sanger founded Planned
Parenthood in 1939 and later became honorary president
of International Planned Parenthood. Drawing from her
second husband's wealth, she established the Margaret
Sanger Research Bureau that financed the development of
the birth-control pill. Gandhi, a man of God, was entirely
self-effacing. He advocated natural family planning and
preached that virtuous temperance should be rooted in
love. "If love is not the law of our being," he declared, "the
whole fabric of my argument falls to pieces."

He called the particular form of temperance he practiced
and preached, *brahmacharya*, a Sanskrit word referring to
perfect control over the appetites and bodily organs. In
1924, Gandhi stated that, fully and properly understood,
temperance, or *brahmacharya*, "signifies control of all the
senses at all times and places in thought, word, and deed." It
includes, yet transcends, sexual restraint. It rules out violence, untruth, hate, and anger. It creates a state of even-
mindedness that allows for self-transformation in God.

Gandhi saw in the use of contraception the potential
for man undoing himself. The virtue of temperance or
brahmacharya is needed, he felt, for man to be truly himself and to allow God to work through him. Therefore,

contraception, which divorces the sexual act from its natural consequence, divides man, separating him from the
meaning of his own actions. For Gandhi, contraception
"simply unmans man":

> I suggest that it is cowardly to refuse to face the conse-
> quences of one's acts. Persons who use contraception will
> never learn the value of self-restraint. They will not need
> it. Self-indulgence with contraceptives may prevent the
> coming of children but will sap the vitality of both men
> and women, perhaps more of men than of women. It is
> unmanly to refuse battle with the devil.

Rome Has Also Spoken
Pope Paul VI echoed many of the thoughts that Gandhi
expounded concerning the evils of contraception. Gandhi
stated that, "As it is, man has sufficiently degraded
woman for his lust, and artificial methods, no matter how
well-meaning the advocates may be, will still *further
degrade her*." Pope Paul VI wrote:

> It is also to be feared that the man, growing used to the
> employment of anti-conception practices, may finally
> lose respect for the woman and, no longer caring for her
> physical and psychological equilibrium, may come to the
> point of considering her as a mere instrument of selfish
> enjoyment, and no longer as his respected and beloved
> companion.[2]

Gandhi advised people to use that particular part of
temperance called "self-restraint" to achieve "self-transformation." Pope Paul VI underscored the importance of

---

[2] Pope Paul VI, Encyclical Letter On Human Life *Humanae Vitae* (1968), no. 17.

"self-mastery" in matters of sexuality (cf. Catechism, 2346). They both spoke of the importance of education and the cooperation of external agencies. Neither was hesitant in identifying the use of contraception as an evil and a disorder. Both saw contraception as an enemy to marriage.

Separate Paths

The distinguished British journalist, Malcolm Muggeridge, long before he became a Roman Catholic, offered a comment in praise of *Humanae Vitae* that may be taken as an apt comment on the 1936 discussion between Gandhi and Sanger:

> One of the things I admired the Church for so much was *Humanae Vitae*. I think it's absolutely right that when a society doesn't want children, when it's prepared to accept eroticism unrelated in any way to its purpose, then it's on the downward path.

The paths of temperance or *brahmacharya* and *eroticism* most assuredly do not move in the same direction. As current history has indicated, the former leads to a *culture of life*, while the latter leads to a *culture of death*.

· SOPHROSYNE ·

In order to understand the virtue of *sophrosyne*,[1] which Plato discusses in Book IV of his *Republic*, one must first know something about the structure and proper functioning of his "tripartite soul." The three parts of the soul, for Plato, are reason, spirit, and appetite. Reason is the ruling principle, appetite is desire, while spirit (*thumos*) is the power that transmits the verdict of reason to the appetite. *Sophrosyne* is precisely the power or virtue that unifies the spirit and appetite under the rule of reason.

Sophrosyne closely resembles temperance, which for the Scholastics is a virtue of the appetite. It unifies the soul as an intermediary agent. Thus, it is alternately translated as soundness, sobriety, or self-control. This "middle part" of the soul, so to speak, which Plato calls "spirit," identifies a human power without which personal integrity could not be a possibility.

No Soul in the Center

Throughout Western history, many influential thinkers have come to the unhappy conclusion that personal integrity is not possible for the specific reason that there is no such thing as an intermediary agent in the human soul

---

[1] *Sophrosyne* can be translated as "control over certain pleasures of the soul." Cf. Allan Bloom, *The Republic of Plato* (New York: Basic Books, 1991), 451.

that could be instrumental in unifying personality. Perhaps the most influential of these thinkers is Sigmund Freud.

Freud postulated reason and appetite (the "superego" and the "id," according to his terminology), but did not envision anything like Plato's "spirit" that could harmonize the two. As a consequence, Freud saw all authority (which emanated from various sources of reason) as essentially oppressive, preventing "desire" (or "instinct") from having its free and unrepressed expression. Freud's *Civilization and Its Discontents* is a rather gloomy dissertation on the unremediable antagonism between the claims of civilization (reason) and the demands of instinct (desire).

For Freud, the impossibility of either the virtue of *sophrosyne* or an integrated personality also creates an antagonism between man and life. Thus, he writes:

> Life, as we find it, is too hard for us; it entails too much pain, too many disappointments, [and] impossible tasks. We cannot do without palliative remedies. . . . There are perhaps three of these means: powerful diversions of interest, which lead us to care little about our misery; substitutive gratifications, which lessen it; and intoxicating substances, which make us insensitive to it.[2]

When Freud wrote these words, he was not thinking about today's TV junkie who dines on media images of worldly possessions while drowning his cares in alcohol. Nonetheless, he would be sympathetically disposed to him. Given the essential antagonism between reason and desire, man can be neither whole nor happy, only distracted.

---

[2] Sigmund Freud, *Civilization and Its Discontents* (London: Hogarth Press, 1957), trans. by Joan Riviere, 25.

Mind Over Media

Freud's pessimism brings to mind the anti-utopian world of Aldous Huxley's *Brave New World* in which drugs substitute for virtue: "You can carry at least half your morality about in a bottle. Christianity without tears—that's what *soma* is." In Freud's words:

> The service rendered by intoxicating media in the struggle for happiness and in keeping misery at a distance is so highly prized as a benefit that individuals and peoples alike have given them an established place in the economics of their libido.

If man is an appetite frustrated by the imposition of repressive authority (reason), the Freudian solution of deflections, substitutions, and intoxicants seems inevitable. The essential problem, however, lies in viewing man in this disintegrated manner in the first place. The unity of the human person is admittedly precarious. In the absence of virtue, man collapses into a collection of warring fragments. Freud did not believe in an integrating virtue, such as *sophrosyne*, because his fascination with the parts of man, particularly *desire*, obscured any appreciation for man's potential wholeness. In fact, Freud sees desire as having a virtual right not to be held back by reason.

You've Been Disconnected

C.S. Lewis, in his brief but penetrating work, *The Abolition of Man*, deplores the modern tendency to remove the "spirit" of man and expect him to continue to function as a man. He upholds the importance of *sophrosyne* when he states that "by his intellect he [man] is mere spirit and by his appetite mere animal," but "it is by this middle element [Plato's "spirit" or *thumos*] that man is man." Just as the king governs his people by his executive, so reason must rule the appetite by means of "spirit"—"the head rules the belly through the chest." In today's world "men without chests" seems to be a commonplace occurrence.

In the absence of *sophrosyne*, man begins to look like a hybrid of contradictory elements. When the liaison officer between cerebral man and visceral man is dismissed, there is little or no prospect for either real unity or personal serenity. Social philosopher Lewis Mumford has remarked that "we have lived to witness the joining in intimate partnership of the automaton and the id." And the psychoanalytic humanist Erich Fromm has observed that "the dream of many people seems to be to combine the emotions of a primate with a computer-like brain." By denying the middle element of man—spirit—man can no longer be whole, indeed, no longer be man.

Family Affair

Christopher Lasch, in his book about the family, entitled, *Haven in a Heartless World*, reminds us that it is the role of the family to mediate the seemingly harsh rules of life with the seemingly irrepressible forces of instinct. The vital role of parents is to see to it that their children grow up to be integrated human beings. Parents are cultivators of the virtue of *sophrosyne*. As parents abandon this role, and as the family breaks down, more and more children are released into the world as disunified, fragmented, and unhappy people.

Reason is only too evident. The computer, in fact, is reason incarnate, a veritable logic machine. Appetite is equally evident. The Age of the Computer is also the Age of Sensation. Hedonism is as prominent a feature of contemporary culture as rationalism. Spirit, however, is not nearly so discernible. And since it remains relatively unattended, the Age of the Computer and the Age of Sensation is also the Age of Anxiety.

Plato looked to music, the arts, and gymnastics as ways of cultivating *sophrosyne*. He may have underestimated the role of loving parents. *Sophrosyne* is more than discipline, which could be of a stoic kind. It is more than temperance, which, as C.S. Lewis has complained, sometimes degenerates into "teetolatism" (for "teetotallers"). Nor is it simply moderation, which can be a dull and dreary affair. *Sophrosyne* is the virtue by which a person becomes an integrated, whole, and vibrant human being. Our choice in life should not be to become a computer-like brain or a trousered ape, but a true, authentic, and balanced human being.

· INTEGRITY ·

At the opposite ends of the moral spectrum are *holiness* and *multiplicity*. This pairing of polar opposites may seem odd at first, but it is solidly biblical. *Holiness* is so named because it represents *wholeness* or unity of personality. God is eminently holy and His saints are holy to the degree they emulate Him. According to traditional orthodox teaching, God, who is "the fullness of Being and of every perfection" (Catechism, no. 213), has the character of *simplicity*. For Saint Augustine, "God is truly and absolutely simple." And for Saint Hilary, "God, who is strength, is not made up of things that are weak; nor is He who is light, composed of things that are dim."

Going to Pieces

Multiplicity is fragmentation, fractionalization, dispersion, and dividedness. It is captured in the colloquial expression "going to pieces." Multiplicity in this sense also corresponds to the notion of *diabolical*, which literally means "going off in opposite directions." In Mark 5:1-20 and Luke 8:26-39, we read about the man who lived in the country of the Gerasenes who was possessed by an unclean spirit. The poor man was out of sorts, to say the least. He would howl and gash himself with stones. Quite literally, he was out of control. His fellow countrymen would bind him with chains and fetters. But he would break the chains asunder, tear the fetters to pieces, and be driven by the devil into the desert.

This poor man submitted himself to Christ, who commanded the unclean spirit to declare its name. "Legion," was the response, "for many devils had entered him" (Lk. 8:30). Christ then allowed the legion of devils to enter a herd of swine, approximately two thousand in all, who then rushed with great violence into the sea and were drowned. This spectacle of mass *disintegration* was indeed terrifying to the swineherds who reported the event to their townsfolk.

Wholeness Next to Godliness

The difference between God and the devil is the difference between *simplicity* and *multiplicity*. We human beings cannot hope to achieve simplicity, but we can achieve integrity and avoid multiplicity.

A favorite theme among twentieth-century writers is the fundamental moral importance of personal integrity. The word they often use to describe this state is *authenticity*. A person should be himself, they insist, and not divide himself into incompatible parts: one for himself and another for the masses.

Because our unity of personality demands the integration of its parts, there is always the possibility that we can break up ("dis-integrate") into discordant pieces. But what are these parts that must be integrated if the person is to be whole? There are many lines along which personality can be unified. There is the integrity between word and deed, friendship and fidelity, private life and public life, mind and body, head and heart. But the integrity that is perhaps most basic to a human being is the one that binds one's *being* to one's *behavior*, *endowment* to *achievement*, or *giftedness* to *response*.

Claiming Our Inheritance

God has given us our inheritance and an inclination toward our destiny. We are free to reject this inheritance because we do not think it is good enough. Thus, we may spend our life envying others whom we judge to be more talented, intelligent, attractive, and so on. Or we may decide not to make the effort of claiming our natural inheritance so as to fulfill our destiny. The great Christian existentialist, Søren Kierkegaard, distinguished these two dispositions, respectively, as the "despair of weakness" and the "despair of defiance."

We need integrity to become who we are, so that we can complement God's gift to us with our gift to Him. Although we often lack integrity in ourselves, we are usually quick to recognize and denounce it in others. So it was with that great cinematic legend of yesteryear, the Lone Ranger's trusty sidekick, Tonto, who instinctively distrusted the "white man" who "spoke with forked tongue." We detest phoniness, hypocrisy, duplicity, double-dealing, and disingenuousness. We admire integrity, though we know that it often comes at a high price.

Specialization and bureaucracy contribute heavily to the process of disintegration. Politics is another area that poses a formidable challenge to anyone who wants to retain his integrity. On the abortion issue, for example, one commonly hears about politicians who are privately opposed but publicly in favor of it.

That's Entertainment?

Charlton Heston stood up at a Time/Warner stockholders' meeting not too long ago and read the shocking lyrics of certain rock songs that passed for "entertainment" in the judgment of that corporation. He said that he expected he would never again be invited to make a film with Warner Brothers and would win many enemies, but that he had a moral obligation to do what he could to start cleaning up some of the filth that is demoralizing contemporary society. He announced to his stunned audience that his integrity meant more to him than his status in the eyes of Time/Warner. As he read the lyrics that were rife with sexism, racism, and violence, "The Time/Warner executives," according to Heston, "squirmed in their chairs and stared at their shoes. They hated me for that." Nonetheless, much good did result from his address.

The sacrifice of fame and fortune, to whatever extent, however, does not compare with the sacrifice of one's integrity. In his impassioned speech to the stockholders, Mr. Heston would have done well to quote Kierkegaard:

> Or can you think of anything more frightful than that it might end with your nature being resolved into a multiplicity, that you really might become many, become, like those unhappy demoniacs, a legion, and you thus would have lost the inmost and holiest thing of all in a man, the unifying power of personality?

· INNOCENCE ·

"How many of you are pro-choice?" she asked her grade-school pupils. Immediately, all hands shot up, except one. "Why are you not pro-choice?" the teacher queried her lone dissenter. "Because I am pro-life," she said, with a confidence that seemed to belie her tender age of seven years. "And why are you pro-life?" the teacher continued. "Because my Mommy and Daddy are pro-life," was the youngster's firm reply. But her stern examiner had not yet completed her line of inquiry. "Suppose your parents were morons?" "Then," said the little girl, and quite emphatically, "I'd be pro-choice."

The teacher's attempt to discredit her pupil's basis for holding a pro-life position obviously backfired. By unintentionally implying that only morons are pro-choice, the child exploited her teacher's logic to her own advantage. This exchange, which actually took place at a Toronto elementary school, is a parable for the unworkability of the pro-choice rhetoric. The child's words are far wiser than she could possibly have suspected.

Words Aren't Enough

Having loving parents is not a bad basis for being pro-life. By contract, having a manipulative teacher is not a good basis for being pro-choice. By listening to her parents, the young girl was responding to people, who in turn, form their pro-life convictions by responding to a reality, namely, the human value of unborn human life. Her conforming colleagues, however, were not responding to a reality as much as reacting to a word. Who would not be in favor of choice?! Who would not be in favor of green? But a green face! Everyone loves a surprise, until it reveals itself to be terribly bad news.

The teacher, who apparently is willing to abandon pedagogy for demagoguery, does not inform her students what the particular choice of abortion actually entails. Had the teacher asked, "How many of you are in favor of removing all rights to life from unborn babies so that their own mothers are free to kill them?" one would suppose that no normal seven-year-old could possibly endorse such a thoroughly heartless position. Being pro-choice can be maintained only by suppressing reality, while reacting, instead, to the sweet sound of certain abstract words. As in advertising, what is sold is not the steak but the sizzle.

Life Is Not a Dream

I have just finished reviewing Michael Schooyans' new book, *The Totalitarian Trend of Liberalism*. The author is a professor at the University of Louvain, Belgium, and has had a brilliant and eventful academic career. Although his book is highly technical and represents a great deal of research, the main point is very much in harmony with our seven-year-old's outlook. Just as the ideology of choice uses words to evoke dreams, so does the ideology of liberalism. *Choice* draws us into fantasy; *life* leads to reality. *Liberalism* is a world suspended from the gritty facts of reality, whereas *liberty* is an important dimension (though certainly not the only one) of human existence. Thus, Schooyans labors to show us that we should use our liberty realistically, in the

service of life, and not employ a smokescreen of liberal ideology to avoid it.

Grade-school children should be fed fairy tales, not ide-
ologies. The former are infinitely more realistic. A good
fairy tale will always make sure to include some frightfully
wicked individual (whose iniquities cannot be justified on
the basis of choice alone). Reality is full of them, and the
wise student will come to realize that dealing with reality
demands a great deal of courage and various other virtues.
But an ideology, such as the one pro-choicers proselytize,
invites people to withdraw into a dreamworld where they
imagine that everyone is free and no one is ever con-
strained. In such a frictionless world, how could one ever
determine whether anyone is a moron? Could we determine
that anyone is a moron apart from how he relates to an
undebatable reality? Could not a real moron (if he were
well-coached) always excuse his peculiar behavior simply by
claiming that he is pro-choice? In a world of choice without
measure, how could we find justification for calling even a
moron, "moron"?

Get Real

Dreams are popular because they are undemanding. But
a good teacher does not want his students to fall asleep in
class. Realities, on the other hand, are unpopular precisely
because they are demanding. Yet the very purpose of education is to prepare students so that they can better meet
the rigorous demands of reality. Life is challenging;
"choice" is evasive.

Education should arouse us from a dreamlike trance in
which we are mesmerized by agreeable, though unrealistic,
thoughts. In this regard, returning to our opening anecdote,
the tables are turned. We may have more to learn, at least

about "choice" and "life," from a seven-year-old girl than from her salaried and certified teacher. Out of the mouths of babes!

Did the Shepherd of Hermas, in the second century, have any inkling into how prophetic he was when he uttered these words: "Hold fast to simplicity of heart and innocence. Yes, be as infants who do not know the wickedness that destroys the life of men."

· JUBILANCE ·

Each year at Christmastime we read diatribes in the press about how the Yuletide Season has become over-commercialized. The indictment is true, I suppose, but the problem is that such journalism has become as tedious as it is predictable. By far, the more arresting aspect of Christmas is connected with its persistence. Underneath the fuss, the mall madness, and the curious practice of buying things you do not want for people you do not like with money you do not have, is something that will not go away—something, in fact, that is timeless.

Christmas, even for non-Christians, is a feast. Now it is proper to a feast that we welcome and approve the luxury of excess. We shop, eat, drink, and even sing a little too much. But a feast does not frown upon excess; it embraces it with intemperate merriment. This is something that Christians heartily endorse, but is anathema to the puritanical mind. It was the Puritans in Great Britain who did away with the observance of Christmas by law in 1643. Their Puritan counterparts in the American colonies soon copied these English laws.

War and Feast

Excess itself is connected with jubilation. One cannot be, nor should even try to be, moderately jubilant. The jubilant person is not tepid. That would be an oxymoron if there ever was one. Jubilation, in turn, is connected with the transcendent. We are jubilant when we celebrate things that are timeless, things that belong to the realm of the divine. This is why Christmas, which has persisted for two thousand years, must be understood, even on a universal level, as a religious event. It is the expression of the ineradicability of man's religious impulse.

We need festivals, festivities, and feasts because we need to thank God for bestowing upon us the gifts of life and love. The holidays in which we celebrate mere mortals— Victoria Day in Canada, Presidents' Day in the United States—soon degenerate into nothing more than protracted weekends. A real feast celebrates what is immortal. And this is why excess and jubilation have their essential places.

A number of years ago, the world-renown scholar, Josef Pieper, presented the Hagey Lectures at the University of Waterloo. The gist of his presentation was that the alternative to a true feast, in which we give thanks to the transcendent, is war. It is a striking thesis. If we have no one to thank for who we are and what we have, we will become so engrossed in the business of business, the competitive rat race, that we will soon be preparing for war. "Cut off from worship of the divine," Pieper writes in his classic work, *Leisure the Basis of Culture*, "leisure becomes laziness and work inhuman."

The persistence, the timelessness, the excess, and the jubilation associated with the Christmas season all point away from war and toward the divine.

Heaven Belongs to These

But there is something very special about the feast that is Christmas. Those whose hearts most rejoice in Christmas are children. Children, of course, have little interest in work or in business, but they do possess a remarkably strong affinity for the supernatural. "Genius," wrote Charles

Baudelaire, "is the rediscovery of childhood." For the poet William Wordsworth, "Heaven lies about in our infancy!"

Christmas itself is about a child who enters a world of darkness with the promise of salvation. It is, therefore, about innocence, humility, love, hope, community, generosity, and so forth. If we respond with a similar multitude of virtues, it is small wonder that our celebrations tend to be extravagant and excessive. Children seem to understand this instinctively, and their enthusiasm for Christmas is boundless. Santa Claus is an endearing image of this profligate munificence.

Christmas is a time, then, for all of us to be at least children at heart. We welcome abundance with the abundance we feel in our hearts. We do not want to be absorbed in a world of work. The antithesis of Christmas is poor Sisyphus who is condemned to rolling his rock, endlessly, meaninglessly. Sisyphus is totally absorbed by his function, never pausing in his work, and never gathering any fruit from his labor.

We should have less anxiety about Christmas being overcommercialized than forgetting why we need to have a feast. The feast is a kind of spiritual resuscitation that brings us back to the living realization that there is more to life than work and more to love than pleasure. Christmas invites us to express our gratitude with reckless merriment and jubilant praise: "Merry Christmas! God bless us, every one!"

· UPRIGHTNESS ·

For the LORD *is righteous, he loves righteous deeds;*
the upright of heart shall behold his face.
—Psalm 11:7

While there are many allusions to the virtue of "upright-ness" in the Old Testament, it is scarcely ever mentioned in today's secular world. Uprightness, nonetheless, remains an essential virtue, and one, in fact, that genuinely epitomizes the good man.

According to the Old Testament, uprightness is a rich and complex notion. It refers to integrity, justice, honesty, fidelity, mercy, and sincerity. Yet it is more than these. It also demands a harmony between moral principles and personal wholeness. But most of all, uprightness is a manifestation of God's will. The person who is upright presents God to the world. As a consequence, God honors the upright man who honors Him: "Truly God is good to the upright" (Ps. 73:1); "the upright enjoy his favor" (Prov. 14:9); "the tent of the upright will flourish" (Prov. 14:11).

Good Posture

While the world does not embrace uprightness in its biblical wholeness, it does cling to vestiges of uprightness. R.K. Douglas, in his book, *Confucianism and Taoism*, refers to the "Sage," who "maintains a perfect uprightness and pursues the heavenly way without the slightest deflection." Buckingham palace guards are at least visual embodiments of unswerving uprightness, as are, for example, military personnel who officiate at funeral ceremonies.

The American cinema in the 1940s and 50s offered images of uprightness in the form of the cowboy who sat tall in the saddle. Gary Cooper in *High Noon* (a time when both hands on the clock are in the upright position) personifies, though without a relationship with God, a character of fearless and unimpeachable uprightness.

On the other hand, what presently captures the secular posture is the pungent image in the title of the book by culture critic Robert Bork, *Slouching Towards Gomorrah*. Jacques Maritain had complained earlier in *The Peasant of the Garonne* of certain Catholics "kneeling before the world."

Making a Stand

Uprightness differs from "righteousness," according to Scripture, more by emphasis than by distinctiveness of meaning. One emphasizes the person who is moral, the other emphasizes the morality apart from the person. Thus, David can say: "I will praise thee with an upright heart, when I learn thy righteous ordinances" (Ps. 119:7).

There are abundant references in the Old Testament linking uprightness to the heart: "My words declare the uprightness of my heart" (Job 33:3); "My shield is with God, who saves the upright in heart" (Ps. 7:10); "in the uprightness of my heart I have freely offered all these things" (1 Chron. 29:17).

The "heart" symbolizes both spontaneity and wholeness. Uprightness is not a matter of mere intellect. It represents the unity of body and mind, faith and action, posture and practice. Here the notion of "rectitude" fittingly captures the dignity and moral impeccability of the upright person.

By contrast, the serpent in the Garden of Eden crawls on its belly. Cowards, and other less upright people, are "cowering," "devious," "crooked," "low," "shaking," "shuddering," "trembling," and so on. Rectitude and posture cannot be emphasized enough. Christ on the Cross is the ultimate symbol and redemptive image of the worth and power of uprightness. Christ remains upright, though it means His agony and death.

Outrunning Adversity

The 1924 Olympic Games in Paris offered the world a memorable example of uprightness, as portrayed in the movie, *Chariots of Fire*. Scotland's Eric Liddle, a theology student, refused to dishonor the Lord's Day by running on that day. Instead, he made an arrangement with his compatriot, Harold Abrams. The two athletes traded events. Liddle agreed to run Abrams' 400-meter race that was scheduled for Tuesday, while Abrams agreed to run the 100 meters that was scheduled for Sunday. Abrams had no religious objection to running on Sunday since, according to his Jewish faith, the Sabbath is Saturday.

The exchange satisfied both their religious beliefs, but put them at a disadvantage competitively inasmuch as they surrendered their best events. Abrams, however, won the 100 meters. No European had ever won a gold medal in that event, and it would be fifty years before one won it again. Liddle, despite the disadvantage he took upon himself, ran the race of his life and won the 400 meters in a new world-record time of 47.6 seconds.

In the days leading up to his victory, the masseur who was officially assigned to care for the British team had come to know and admire Eric Liddle. As Liddle was leaving for Colombes Stadium on the day of his stunning victory, the masseur came up to him and pressed a piece of folded paper into his hand. Later that day, in a quiet moment, Liddle unfolded the paper and read the message it contained: "In the old book it says, 'He that honor me I will honor.' Wishing you the best of success always."

Eric Liddle was a man of inspiring uprightness. His example has not lost its luster with the passing of time. His embodiment of moral rectitude, courage, faith, and victory may be difficult to emulate, but it is impossible to ignore. At the same time, it is also a testimony that God will not abandon the upright man.

· II ·

THE INTER-PERSONAL VIRTUES

· CARE ·

The heart of virtue is love. Love without virtue remains unexpressed. Virtue is the pipeline, so to speak, that taps into the source of love within the person and allows it to be expressed in a loving act. Love is realized in act. Virtue is the channel through which love flows from potency to act, from source to expression, from hope to realization.

The degree of intimacy with love is more evident in some virtues than in others. In the case of courtesy or justice, for example, the degree of intimacy with love may not be readily apparent. But with care, more than with any other virtue, the identification with love is unmistakable. When people care for one another, ministering to each other's needs, as a mother cares for her new baby, a doctor cares for a sick patient, or a teacher cares for a struggling student, the connection between love and virtue is evident. The popular expression "tender loving care" reveals the deep intimacy between the virtue of care and its heart of love. Care, then, is the virtue that is most synonymous with love.

To Care Is Human

A human being is, most fundamentally, one who is called into existence *by* love and called into existence *to* love. Pope John Paul II, therefore, says that "love is the fullest realization of the possibilities inherent in man." Because the virtue of care is so deeply associated with love, it comes the closest of all virtues to coinciding with it. And because love personifies the human being, care is the name that comes closest to revealing his identity.

The inability to care, more than anything else, shows a human being to be inhuman. To care is to express human-ness, to reveal love. Not to care is to place a barrier between oneself and one's own humanity. It is to remain unloving.

Roman mythology teaches that the truest name for the human person is "Care," and offers an imaginative and instructive fable to illustrate how this name came to be chosen:

One day, Care was amusing herself by molding earth into various shapes. She fashioned one shape that especially amused her. Wanting this new form to enjoy life, she beseeched Jupiter to grant it a soul. Jupiter obliged Care by breathing life into the earthly form. Care then requested that this new creature be named after her. When Jupiter objected, they asked Saturn, the god of time, to serve as arbiter. Saturn decreed that, when the new creature died, its body had to return to Earth, which was its origin; its soul had to return to its father, Jupiter, who had given it life. But all the time it was alive, it was to be entrusted to Care.

Harvard scholar and poet, Henry Wadsworth Longfellow, who had a great affection for the myths of antiquity, also wrote about the primal place of time and care in the constitution of man. He conceived an image that exquisitely parallels the Roman myth:

> The everyday cares and duties, which men call drudgery, are the weights and counterpoises of the clock of time, giving its pendulum a true vibration, and its hands a regu-lar motion; and when they cease to hang upon the wheels, the pendulum no longer swings, the hands no longer move, and the clock stands still.

The absence of care is the death of personality. Care may seem to be a weight, but in fact it is the counterweight that gives life its balance, its vibrancy, its authenticity.

He Ain't Heavy

Yet the central problem with care is precisely that many view it as drudgery. People long for the so-called "care-free" life, one that exempts them from the burden of having to care for other people, especially the very young and the very old. Yet this "care-free" ideal is infected with ominous implications for abortion and euthanasia. No doubt, caring can be inconvenient on occasion and can place considerable demands on our time. Indeed, the many cares of life can be exhausting. Shakespeare said that we needed sleep to knot up the raveled sleeve of care. And Milton, in "L'Allegro," derided Care as a wrinkled old hag.

Ironically, the virtue that makes us authentically human—caring—often appears so burdensome that a person prefers to be other than who he is. Sluggishness, indifference to others, is therefore commonplace. Thus, Mother Teresa of Calcutta could say, "The greatest disease in the West is not tuberculosis or leprosy; it is being unwanted, unloved, and uncared for."[1]

Despite the horrifying ordeal she experienced at a Nazi concentration camp during World War II, Wanda Poltawska, an advisor for Catholics United for the Faith, has never lost her caring concern for others. As a psychiatrist, she draws from her experience to provide specialized care to others who have suffered from the horrors of war and genocide.

---

[1] Mother Teresa, *Heart of Joy* (Ann Arbor, MI: Servant Books, 1987), 54.

When Pope John Paul II was shot in a failed assassination attempt, the first thing he did upon his release from the hospital was to visit his assailant in prison and pardon him. Even those who contest his words do not challenge his integrity and his abiding care for others—including those who have trespassed against him.

Care does not allow suffering, either in the self or in the other, to prevent love from being expressed. It is the virtue that allows love to overcome its first and most fundamental obstacle, namely, inconvenience. It is never too inconvenient to love as long as one has care. "He's not heavy," said the lad who seemed to be struggling under the burden of the young tike he was carrying. "He's my brother."

· COURTESY ·

Marshall McLuhan once described the newspaper as "orchestrated discontinuity." It is difficult to ascertain how much influence the newspaper has had on life, but life itself has become an increasingly exasperating experience of "orchestrated discontinuity."

I recently drove into a filling station to fill my gas tank and take advantage of its new at-the-pump method of payment that dispenses with the need of a human cashier. The computer, however, did not recognize my credit card and therefore did not authorize its use. I was therefore obliged, though not unhappily, to deal with a human being. She explained to me that, in her opinion, the reason the computer did not accept my card was because it may have had a nick or scratch on it. "These machines are very sensitive," she said, in an understanding tone that seemed to reflect the voice of considerable experience. We examined the card. I always kept it snug in my leather wallet, giving it a private pouch that was free from any possible rough contact with other cards. Yet, there it was, a tiny abrasion on the upper edge, enough, presumably, to make it unrecognizable to the sensitive eye of the computer.

Close to the cash register was a special display of a new and apparently quite "hot" video—*The Best of Jerry Springer*. The word *best*, of course, is better understood as meaning *worst*. And here is the "orchestrated discontinuity": While technicians are laboring to make our machines more sensitive, television producers are laboring equally hard to make their programming more coarse. It has been estimated by certain authorities in the business that the *Jerry Springer Show* exceeds the now-defunct *Geraldo Rivera Show* in sheer coarseness by a factor of at least ten. Yet even this new nadir in coarseness has been surpassed by the video.

Air-Conditioned Nightmare

We are obliged to keep our credit cards immaculate out of deference to sensitive machinery. But, when it comes to human interaction, at least in the popular style exhibited on the immensely successful *Jerry Springer Show*, gross insensitivity to other people's feelings is the order of the day.

We now live, as the playwright Arthur Miller has pointed out, "in an air-conditioned nightmare." We treat our neighbor in a manner that would not be tolerated by a sensitive computer. Another way of putting it is to say that we are misplacing sensitivity. Human beings are incomparably more sensitive than any kind of machinery. The computer does not really care if it is used, abused, or ignored. But human beings do. And profoundly. Yet we consider it progress to make machines that are more and more sensitive, while we note the marked increase in crudeness that takes place between human beings. We feel a growing obligation not to bruise our credit cards, while we observe that bruising other people's feelings is becoming a national pastime.

Persons, Not Machines

What is missing in our era of machine-efficiency is courtesy. There is no point in being courteous to a machine. The machine is programmed for efficiency, not civility. Human beings need to be acknowledged as having a value that has absolutely nothing to do with efficiency. They need to be honored as human beings. Courtesy does this. It is the entrance-level virtue that acknowledges that the other human being is worthy of being honored simply because he is a human being. Courtesy may or may not lead to friendship, but it is the first virtue in the catalog of human virtues that one can express to a complete stranger without risk of impropriety.

There is no point in greeting a machine or saying "hello" to it. Its sensitivity is wholly mechanical. Human beings, unlike machines, have an inherent dignity. They need to be reminded of this dignity, less they forget they possess it.

Our ability to recognize that another human being is a human being is not impaired by the fact that he is imperfect in some way. A society of unblemished, beautiful people is one in which common courtesy would be unnecessary. The ideal for a credit card is not the ideal for a human being. "I will not recognize you unless you are unflawed," is the most discourteous attitude one could have for another human being. It represents the failure to acknowledge the dignity that is inherent in each one of us.

Ladies and Gentlemen

Courtesy in the entrance-level virtue that allows strangers suddenly to feel that they are kindred spirits. It is also the foundation on which other virtues might be established, such as kindness, thoughtfulness, amicability, and generosity. No true and lasting human relationship can begin without the virtue of courtesy. It appears at the beginning of a relationship (should we call it a *relationship?*) and abides throughout it. It is expressed to both the stranger and to the intimate. It is the needed antidote to our world of machine-efficiency. It reminds us of our distinctive humanity and invites us to follow its beckoning course. Its sensitivity is always an accepting one, greeting the poor and the afflicted with equal temperament along with the affluent and the healthy. It offers the smile of recognition and the possibility of friendship. It costs nothing, and can, at times, save us from despair.

· KINDHEARTEDNESS ·

There are three theological virtues: faith, hope, and charity. And there are four cardinal virtues: prudence, justice, temperance, and fortitude. This is only too well-known. I would like to introduce what I call the three "infectious virtues": kindheartedness, lightheartedness, and warmheartedness. They are infectious because they tend to reproduce themselves in the people they greet. They mirror themselves in other people's souls. They have a directness and an amiability that cause their beneficiaries to want to reciprocate in kind. Kindheartedness engenders kindness, lightheartedness engenders cheerfulness, and warmheartedness engenders sympathy.

The heart is the source and the form of all moral virtues. But in the infectious virtues, the heart manifests itself with more immediacy than do any of the other virtues. In fact, someone who has these virtues elicits a positive response from people without having to express them in a deed. It is as if their presence in the heart is enough to make them heartfelt. Hence, they are also the "visceral virtues," communicating to others through the silent eloquence of the body. They are the virtues that the writer is comfortable with, more than the philosopher is, since they show how a good habit can manifest itself in the body language of its possessor so well that it becomes palpable to others.

The good heart should have three qualities: it should be kind, not callous; light, not heavy; warm, not cold. By comparison, justice, courage, generosity, and so on, appear to be somewhat overbroad and abstract. We may not recognize that a man is sincere by merely looking at him. But this is not the case with the triad of "infectious virtues." We literally feel their kindness, cheer, and warmth.

Kindheartedness is unique in that it is the one virtue that is most likely to reproduce its image in another person. In other words, it is the most infectious of the three, the one most likely to be imitated, the one most likely to be passed on.

Get the Ball Rolling

Some time ago a UCLA drama student performed a scene from *Annie Get Your Gun* at a bon voyage party for one of her professors. After the performance, she was standing at the buffet when a man, whom she did not know, approached her and told her how much he enjoyed her routine. He kindly asked her what she intended to do with the rest of her life. The young student, who was operating at that time on little more than hope and dreams, informed him that she hoped to go to New York some day and make a career for herself on stage. When he asked her what was stopping her, she explained that she barely had enough money to get back to Los Angeles, let alone to go to New York. In truth, she, as well as her sister, mother, and grandmother, had, at various times, been living on welfare.

The man smiled and offered to loan her one thousand dollars to get her started. He insisted, however, on three conditions. First, if she met with success, she would repay the loan without interest in five years. Second, she would never reveal his identity. And finally, she would one day "pass the kindness along to help some other person in similar circumstances." The stranger's kindheartedness was so striking that the young aspirant was convinced, as she put it, "that the good Lord was giving me a strong and unmistakable push."

Tell No One

She accepted the money, went to New York, and became a success. Five years to the day, she paid her benefactor back. Nonetheless, the extraordinary kindness of this man, coupled with his express wish to remain anonymous, baffled her. Then one day, while looking for the Lord's Prayer in a recently published translation of the Bible, the following words from Matthew 6:2-4 seemed to leap off the page:

> Thus, when you give alms, sound no trumpet before you, as the hypocrites do. . . . But when you give alms, do not let your left hand know what your right hand is doing, so that your alms may be in secret; and your Father who sees in secret will reward you.

A gift is marred when its giver seeks praise. The truly kindhearted person simply wants to give, and has absolutely no interest in being congratulated for his efforts. His gift is pure, unalloyed by the dross of egoism. As far as the third condition is concerned, the now successful entertainer admits to "passing the kindness along to others," but secretly and anonymously, of course.

Oh yes, the name of the successful artist. She is none other than star of stage, screen, and television—Miss Carol Burnett!

Have you had a kindness shown? Pass it on;
'Twas not given for thee alone, Pass it on;
Let it travel down the years,
Let it wipe another's tears,
'Til in Heaven the deed appears—
Pass it on.

—*Pass It On*
Rev. Henry Burton

· LIGHTHEARTEDNESS ·

Lightheartedness is a most suitable virtue for man since he is essentially a lighthearted being. He is a lighthearted being who has fallen from grace and aspires to rise again. He is caught between the elemental forces of *grace* and *gravity*, struggling to reclaim his lightness and overcome the heaviness of his existence and the world around him. This may be why G.K. Chesterton held that in the great triad of Christian virtues—humility, activity, and cheerfulness—cheerfulness is the most important of all. There is no more striking and startling a paradox concerning Chesterton, who is said to be the "master of the paradox," than the fact that this man of conspicuous corpulence was also a man of cherubic cheerfulness. "Angels fly," he wrote in *Orthodoxy*, "because they can take themselves lightly."

Chesterton himself could soar because he did not take himself seriously. Too much concern for one's ego, or *pride*, he once said, results in "the falsification of fact by the introduction of self." Christian humility demands the "subtraction" of *myself* in order to see things as they are in *themselves*. The humble Christian is then free to undertake his appointed task or activity in a spirit of lighthearted cheerfulness. When Ebenezer Scrooge, of Charles Dickens' *A Christmas Carol*, finally unburdened himself from his weighty ego, he could almost fly: "I am as light as a feather, I am as happy as an angel, I am as merry as a schoolboy."

The heart that is light defies gravity and flies on the wings of levity. Cheerfulness is the natural expression of a person's lightheartedness. John Ruskin, an essayist, critic, and reformer, believed it was an essential virtue:

> Cheerfulness is as natural to the heart of a man in strong health, as color to his cheek; and wherever there is habitual gloom, there must be either bad air, unwholesome food, improperly severe labor, or erring habits.

"A light heart lives long," adds Shakespeare.

Hold onto Your Hats!

The Czech writer, Milan Kundera, titled his celebrated novel *The Unbearable Lightness of Being*. The *lightness* to which he referred, however, was really *weightlessness*. Astronauts who experience *weightlessness* do not *fly*, they merely roll about. Chesterton's lightness is upward, not circular. He could have justifiably called his autobiography *The Enjoyable Lightness of Being*. When another dispirited European writer, Franz Kafka, read Chesterton, he exclaimed, "He is so gay, one might almost believe he had found God." From Kafka this is high praise, indeed.

Chesterton's lightheartedness by no means was empty-headedness. He was not facetious. His cheerfulness never obscured his intelligence. It was his clear intelligence, in fact, that allowed him to see how reckless disregard could be so hilarious. Consider his rebuttal of socialism:

> There might be people who prefer to have their hats leased out to them every week. Or wear their neighbors' hats in rotation to express the idea of comradeship. Or possibly to crowd under one very large hat to represent an even larger, cosmic conception. But most of them feel that something is added to the dignity of men when they put on their *own* hats.

It is interesting to note that disciples of the socialist Saint-Simon wore a special waistcoat that could neither be put on nor taken off unassisted. In their zeal to express comradeship, they lost sight of practical common sense. Chesterton could not be weighed down either by ego or by ideology. Nor was he weighed down by the realization that "the river of human nonsense flows on forever." Nor was he daunted by the unfulfilled dreams of Christianity: "The Christian ideal has not been tried and found wanting. It has been found difficult; and left untried."

Rose-Colored Glasses

Concerning opinion polls, Chesterton was remarkably ahead of his time. They are like lampposts, he commented, "that drunks use more for support than for illumination." "A light touch is the mark of strength," he said. But for him it was also a mark of wit. He was rather rotund, but bore the slights of others with typical lightheartedness. A woman once chided him for not being a combatant in the war. "Why aren't you out in the front?" she asked. "Ma'am," he retorted, "if you'd just step this way, you will see that I am out in the front." To George Bernard Shaw, who said to him, "If I were as fat as you, I would hang myself," Chesterton calmly answered by saying, "If I had a mind to kill myself, I would use you as the rope."

Because he saw the lightness in the nature of everything, he could cheerfully avoid anything that was base. "Variability is one of the virtues of woman," he wrote. "It obviates the crude requirements of polygamy. If you have a good wife you are sure to have a spiritual harem." Thus, he could also hold that "purity is the only atmosphere for passion."

Chesterton's heart was light because his hopes were high. As a Christian, he had much to be cheerful about. "If there were no God," he quipped, "there would be no atheists." Another of his quotes reveals his wit: "The Bible tells us to love our neighbors and also our enemies; probably because generally they are the same people."

Eyes on the Goal

"Adventure," he once remarked, "is the voluntary acceptance of discomfort." Life itself is the greatest of all adventures, but its discomforts are always less than its joys. For it sets man on a search that leads to a discovery that makes everything worthwhile. Chesterton found it all worthwhile, comparing it to the journey to Bethlehem:

> Divinity and infancy do definitely make a sort of epigram which a million repetitions cannot turn into a platitude. Bethlehem is emphatically a place where extremes meet. That tense sense of crisis which still tingles in the Christmas story and even in every Christmas celebration accentuates the idea of a search and discovery.

· WARMHEARTEDNESS ·

Warmheartedness embraces a multitude of virtues, including sympathy, kindness, congeniality, gentleness, and care. We do not expect young people to exhibit warmheartedness. It is a virtue for those who are seasoned in virtue. According to J.P. Marquand, "There is a certain phase in the life of the aged when the warmth of the heart seems to increase in direct proportion with years." Warmheartedness is the soft glow of love, winning over people's trust and rendering them comfortable in an intimate, often domestic, environment.

Cold as Vice

On the other hand, we know only too well how age can harden people, turning them into cranky, crusty, crotchety, cantankerous, "grumpy old men." Life is a drama, ambiguous and uncertain. If we are fortunate and live long enough to enter our "golden years," we have no assurance whatsoever that we will arrive at that noble estate without being cursed by coldheartedness. The entire thrust of Charles Dickens' classic, *A Christmas Carol*, is to warm up the frosty heart of Ebenezer Scrooge. Early in the story, Dickens describes his character as follows:

> The cold within him froze his old features, nipped his pointed nose, shriveled his cheek, stiffened his gait, made his eyes red, his thin lips blue, and spoke out shrewdly in his grating voice. A frosty rime was on his head, and on

his eyebrows, and his wiry chin. He carried his own low temperature always with him; he iced his office in the dog days; and didn't thaw it one degree at Christmas.

Dante's Ninth Circle of Hell is an icy lake. Scrooge was headed in that direction until his heart started to heat up. And when it did, it burst into a paroxysm of love and generosity. If warmheartedness is the channel, love is its furnace. Philosopher Dietrich von Hildebrand speaks of "the peculiar quality of expansive warmheartedness which belongs to pure love." He also points out how easy it is for lust and any of the other deadly sins to cause the heart to atrophy and loose its warmth. A heart of vice is a heart of ice.

Temperature Rising
Shakespeare's *The Life of Timon of Athens* is Dickens' tale told in reverse. Timon is a person of extravagant generosity. He gives his wealth to his friends until he has nothing left. But when he asks his beneficiaries for a little financial help, they all refuse. His heart then turns cold. He is now consumed by hatred for all humanity. He says of his ungrateful associates, "Their blood is caked, 'tis cold, it seldom flows; 'Tis lack of kindly warmth they are not kind." Timon dies at the end of the play, alone and miserable.

The warm heart has the capacity to warm others, just as a source of heat warms its immediate surrounding. A warm heart can touch other hearts and ignite them in the process. The heart of Jesus not only warms, but burns. After talking with Jesus on the road to Emmaus, the two companions say to each other: "Did not our hearts burn within us while he talked to us on the road, while he opened to us the scriptures?" (Lk. 24:32).

One of the endearing features of the warmhearted person is that he manifests his virtue even prior to its enactment. The virtue of warmheartedness, like modesty, is recognized apart from its being expressed in action. Its "temperature" alone is sufficient to make its presence felt. This is the case with any personal feature that has warmth, whether the warmth is in the heart, the eyes, the words, the smile, or the laughter.

Heartwarming Gift

Just as, according to the old saying, "who splits wood warms twice," the warmhearted person engenders warmheartedness in others. Marriage is a relationship that demands that the spouses warm each other's hearts.

A friend of mine went to church and prayed that her husband would relate to her with a little more warmth. She happened to be the only person at the church that particular evening who was not with her spouse. This made her situation all the more poignant. To feel closer to her husband, she removed her wedding ring from her finger and held it in her hand. She then offered her petition, in silence and with hope.

Upon returning home, she was greeted at the door by her husband. He asked her, in warm tones, "You look tired, darling. Can I make you a cup of tea?"

When we warm up people's drinks, we can be taking an important step in warming their hearts. We have house-warmings in the hope that these dwelling places will warm the hearts of all of its future inhabitants and guests. The physical closely neighbors the spiritual. This is "global warming" in the best sense of the expression. "Shall not my heart's warmth not nurse thee into strength?" asks the poet, Robert Browning.

Another character of Dickens, Jowl, in *The Old Curiosity Shop*, boasted that "Experience has never put a chill upon my warmheartedness." It may have been an idle boast for Jowl, who was a rather vain fellow, but it remains an attainable ideal for the rest of us. To remain warmhearted despite the surrounding chills is a most desirable and exalted virtue that can benefit us all. We can all grow warmer with age.

· KINDNESS ·

Aunt Tilly was vacationing in Ireland. Unaccustomed to operating her rented car, and distracted by the fair sights of the Emerald Isle, she experienced the embarrassing misfortune of running out of gas precisely at the moment she stopped at an intersection. Not knowing what to do, she remained frozen at the wheel for some time. The truck driver behind her, after witnessing the traffic lights pass through several cycles, finally decided to take action. He sauntered over to Aunt Tilly's car, leaned his large frame toward her open window, and stated, in as restrained a manner as possible, "Would you be lookin' for a different shade of green, ma'am?"

Putting Anger Away

Kindness is being gentle, thoughtful, helpful, and forgiving at times when it would be so easy to be angry. It also displays the same virtues when the sheer inconvenience of the situation would seem to justify noninvolvement. Kindness much prefers considerateness to anger, and leaps enthusiastically over barriers of inconvenience. The kind person persists in behaving humanly no matter how irresistibly circumstances may tempt him to behave otherwise.

It is only too evident that Christians should be ambassadors of kindness. Saint Paul advises in Ephesians 4:31:

Let all bitterness and wrath and anger and clamor and slander be put away from you, with all malice, and be kind to one another, tenderhearted, forgiving one another, as God in Christ forgave you.

Saint Peter offers similar advice:

So put away all malice and all guile and insincerity and envy and all slander. Like newborn babes, long for the pure spiritual milk, that by it you may grow up to salvation; for you have tasted the kindness of the Lord (1 Pet. 2:1-3).

Milk and Honey

Kindness is the honey that dulls the sting of unkindness when we receive it from another. A kind word can conquer anger, calm the spirit, and even start a friendship.

Christians should be kind. But kindness is not exclusively Christian. Rather it is as broad and old as humanity. The Greek playwright Sophocles alluded to the naturalness of kindness when he said, "Kindness gives birth to kindness." The Roman emperor Marcus Aurelius understood the personal as well as the social benefits of kindness. "Ask thyself daily," he wrote, "to how many ill-minded persons thou hast shown a kind disposition." Goethe viewed kindness as the "golden chain by which society is bound together." The fact that the word kindness is derived from the Old English gecynde, meaning natural, is a good indication that kindness is a very natural virtue. Shakespeare's immortal and oft-quoted phrase, "the milk of human kindness" (Macbeth) also attests to the naturalness of kindness, especially with regard to its manner of nourishment.

Random Acts

In the contemporary world, we commonly hear reference to "random acts of kindness." The expression was coined, presumably, to counteract "random acts of violence." Nonetheless, acts of kindness are not fully themselves if they are random and impersonal. They should be well-placed and personal. "How truly is a kind heart a fountain of gladness," wrote Washington Irving, "making everything in its vicinity to freshen into smiles." No other virtue is better identified with the heart. *Kindness* and *kindheartedness* are synonymous, as are *kind* and *kindhearted*.

Small acts of watchful kindness are seldom performed in vain. And they have a marvelous proclivity for engendering successive acts of kindness. Moreover, kindness is versatile in its manner of expression. The kind look, gesture, or word can be as beneficial as the kind deed.

The expressions of kindness may be simple and undramatic. The results, however, can be decisive and most dramatic. The following story has circulated through the newsprint media: A young man named Mark was trying to negotiate his way home one day with his arms full of paraphernalia he had just taken from his high school locker. The inevitable happened. He tripped. Suddenly, his precious cargo was no longer in his arms but scattered on the sidewalk. A Good Samaritan bystander, a student from the same high school, stopped and helped his distraught neighbor. A small act of kindness, undramatic and unpretentious. A conversation ensued and, before very long, a friendship developed.

When the time was ripe, Mark explained to his new friend that the reason he cleaned out his locker was because he did not want to leave a mess behind for someone else. He had saved up enough of his mother's sleeping pills to put himself to sleep permanently. He was going home to kill himself when an act of unexpected kindness gave his plans and his life a new direction. Kindness, truly, can save lives.

> In success we see a silhouette,
> The outline of an unknown story;
> But kindness is a coronet
> That holds the heart in glory.

· DECENCY ·

I n the 1937 film *Gone With the Wind*, Clark Gable shocked a nation of moviegoers when he said to Vivien Leigh, "Frankly, my dear, I don't give a dam(n)." People allowed themselves to be shocked more than was necessary. The original phrase, "I don't give a dam," was actually rather innocuous since the word "dam" referred to a printer's measure and hence to something of very little value.

In 1940, Bertrand Russell's appointment to teach philosophy at the City College of New York was revoked because of his views on sexuality. One magazine epitomized the broad, public outrage against the appointment when it described Lord Russell as "a desiccated, divorced, and decadent advocate of sexual promiscuity."

While we can take some measure of pride today for being more tolerant and less prissy, we have reason to wonder whether we have become so jaded that nothing at all shocks us any longer. Hugh Hefner and others have dedicated their careers to convincing their public that lust has nothing to do with shame. After Madonna and Howard Stern, adult videos and escort services, royal and presidential scandals, is there anything left that has the power to provoke in us a sense of moral outrage?

Miami Virtue?

William Bennett's recent book, *The Death of Moral Outrage: Bill Clinton and the Assault on American Ideals*, sounds an alarm to awaken people to the dangers of becoming morally numb. For too many people, sexual shenanigans that should shock people are systematically transposed into entertainment fare. What was once morally outrageous is now merely good copy. It is "Miami Vice" we want to watch, not "Miami Virtue." And many seem to live according to the maxim that vice is nice, but virtue can hurt you.

Washington, DC's mayor, Marion Barry, was photographed smoking crack cocaine. After his release from prison, he was promptly reelected. His drug habits were more cool than shocking, more amusing than outrageous.

Woody Allen's 1989 movie, *Crimes and Misdemeanors*, is about how to hire a hit man to "take out" a nagging mistress without ruffling your conscience or compromising your social status. Taking a woman out once referred to showing her a good time. Times have certainly changed. The deeper question is: "Has moral man changed in the process?"

Uncommon Decency

To a significant degree, virtue has now acquired a bad name. For the young, it seems to be the opposite of having fun. For older people, it appears to be a symbol of lost values that politicians exploit for partisan advantage. For young and old alike, it seems to be a set of arbitrary values that one benighted generation tries to impose on the next.

Do we have an innate moral sense that can never be eradicated? Or can we become so desensitized that nothing can ever shock or offend our moral sensibilities? Is common decency a fundamental virtue? Or is it merely a passing product of social conditioning that fades into oblivion as culture becomes more "enlightened"?

Candle in the Wind

James Q. Wilson, who teaches at UCLA, believes that one of the greatest needs of our time is to get back in touch with our moral sense. He closes his book, *The Moral Sense*, with these words:

> Mankind's moral sense is not a strong beacon of light, radiating outward to illuminate in sharp outline all that it touches. It is, rather, a small candle flame, casting vague and multiple shadows, flickering and sputtering in the strong winds of power and passion, greed, and ideology. But brought close to the heart and cupped in one's hands, it dispels the darkness and warms the soul.[1]

It is difficult to read this passage and not think of "Candle in the Wind," Elton John's moving tribute to Lady Diana. While it may very well be that the world's reaction to the tragic ending of Diana's life was oversentimentalized, there is a deeper truth that may give us hope. Human life is fragile and transitory. Like a candle, it is so easily extinguishable. The "winds" that threaten life are brutal and irrational. So, too, can power and passion, greed, and ideology be brutal and irrational. We are outraged when we see this taking place. The public outpouring of grief and affection over Diana's passing assures us that we do have an operative moral sense. We are moved, and powerfully so, when we witness the unfairness of irrational forces snuffing out a beautiful life. We do not cheer for the hurricane.

---

[1] James Q. Wilson, *The Moral Sense* (New York: Free Press, 1993), 251.

Tolerable Outrage

Our moral sense, including our sense of decency, is still intact, though it is at times obscured by the accumulated debris of layer upon layer of tabloid-type entertainment. We must revitalize our capacity for moral outrage without becoming unduly intolerant, while enjoying forms of entertainment that do not make us jaded.

Decency is still a virtue. It is the ability to recognize and rejoice in things that are delightful and wholesome. It is also the capacity to be shocked when confronted with anything that is truly shocking. It is the sense of what is proper behavior and what are suitable standards for personal and artistic expression.

Though decency is at least regulated by law, it should be most strictly observed by men. Traditionally, people have believed that the vast majority of human beings could be relied upon to be decent enough to behave decently. Legal regulation was assumed to be more unnecessary than unwise—the law, of course, being a poor substitute for virtuous behavior. And thus it should be. Decent behavior should be inspired not by law, but by our own sense of decency.

The commonest way in which our sense of decency is assaulted in the contemporary climate is through vile language. But there is never a season for vile language to be generally acceptable. The words of a seventeenth-century poet, W.D. Roscommon, still apply:

> Immodest words admit of no defense,
> For want of decency is want of sense.

· MODESTY ·

Goodness should not be invisible. It should not be colorless. On the other hand, it should not dazzle or overpower. It should compel, not impel; attract, not attack.

Modesty is the virtue that presents goodness in its proper color: one of elegance rather than affluence, of economy rather than extravagance, naturalness rather than ostentation. "What a power has white simplicity," as Keats has aptly written. Modesty is the virtue that allows one to focus on what is good without being distracted by irrelevant superficialities.

Not for Public Consumption

The modest person is content with living well and performing good deeds without fanfare. For him, life is essential, rewards are superfluous. He believes that nature opens to a wider world, whereas ornamentation stifles. He is always averse to gilding the lily. He is confident without being demure, unpretentious without being self-defeating. He lets his actions and words speak for themselves.

Modesty seems out of step with the modern world. As a rule, people are most eager to impress others by recourse to no end of gimmicks. Those who work in the advertising or cosmetic industries regard modesty as a self-imposed handicap. If "nice guys finish last," people of modesty do not even enter the race. Hollywood, or "Tinsel

Town," as it is appropriately called, is the glamour capital of the world, its chief export being the very antithesis of modesty. It champions style over substance, image over essence.

Despite the arrogance and the artificiality of the modern world, modesty retains an unmatched power. It remains a diamond in the midst of zircons. "In the modesty of fearful duty," wrote Shakespeare, "I read as much as from the rattling tongue of saucy and audacious eloquence" (*A Midsummer Night's Dream*). When modesty speaks, its unvarnished eloquence presents that which is as true, dependable, and genuine. Modesty is concerned with honesty, not deceit.

Unwitting Celebrity

Emily Dickinson exemplifies the paradox that modesty, which is unconcerned about stature and reputation, can actually enlarge them. When she was thirty-two, she sent four of her poems to *The Atlantic Monthly*. The magazine's rejection of them led her to believe that the public was not interested in her poetry. This belief remained with her throughout the rest of her life, and she never submitted any more of her works for publication. Although she wrote some 1,775 poems over the course of her life, only seven of them were published—all anonymously, and most of them surreptitiously by friends who wanted to see them in print.

"Fame is a fickle thing," she wrote, "men eat of it and die." As she stated in a letter to a literary critic whom she admired, "My Barefoot Rank is better." Her own modest world was broad enough to fill her heart: "A modest lot . . . is plenty! Is enough." It was her destiny: "I meant to have modest needs, such as content and heaven." She did not require much to be transported from one realm to another. A book was sufficient—"How frugal is the chariot that bears the human soul."

A contemporary American theologian of hers, by the name of Nathaniel Emmons, may have written the perfect summation of Dickinson's triumphant modesty when he said: "Make no display of your talents or attainments; for everyone will clearly see, admire, and acknowledge them, so long as you cover them with the beautiful veil of modesty."

One such admirer was the head of a Catholic religious order who confessed: "I bless God for Emily—some of her writings have had a more profound influence on my life than anything else that anyone has ever written." The general consensus recognizes her as one of America's greatest poets, and the greatest of America's women poets. Moreover, she touched people who ordinarily do not care much for poetry. As one critic put it, she is supremely the poet of those who "never read poetry."

Depth of Character

One of the most basic and vexing problems in moral education is how to make virtue more attractive than vice. In this regard, modesty plays a key role. Modesty is inherently attractive because it invites one to examine the quiet depth of what is there. Display is not as attractive as it is conspicuous. But what is merely conspicuous is often shallow. It is only natural for people to lift up the modest and be turned away by the proud.

The modesty of the following lines that encapsulate Emily Dickinson's life provide a good illustration of the singularly attractive power of modesty:

This is my letter to the World,
That never wrote to Me—
The simple News that Nature told—
With tender Majesty.

Her Message is committed
To Hands I cannot see—
For love of Her—sweet countrymen—
Judge tenderly—of Me.

· COMPASSION I ·

Every virtue has its bogus pretenders. Foolhardiness passes for courage, timidity for prudence, apathy for patience, obsequiousness for courtesy, and credulity for faith. But there is no counterfeit that is more successful in obscuring the genuine article, especially in the present era, than false compassion.

Compassion is not a new virtue, although many employ it with the kind of wide-eyed excitement that might suggest they had discovered it. It is cited many times in Sacred Scripture, both in the Old and New Testaments. Saint Augustine, in his *Confessions*, written in the early fifth century, discussed the fraternal compassion we owe to others and advised that we should prefer to find nothing in them that would elicit our compassion. Saint Bernard, in the twelfth century, said that Christ is our primary teacher of compassion because He willed His passion so that we could learn compassion. Saint Thomas Aquinas, in the thirteenth century, wrote about how our compassion can mitigate the suffering of a friend.

What a Pity!

History has taught us enough about the meaning of compassion so as to leave us with little excuse for confusing it with pity. Compassion, which is rooted in love, takes on the pain of the sufferer, but with the hope that some positive good will emerge from this shared suffering. Pity, on the other hand, which is more closely associated with an aesthetic sensibility than with love, is devoid of hope. This is why a sufferer welcomes compassion but despises pity. "I don't want your pity!" is a poignant cry that implies the futility of pity. And yet, pitilessness, which is insensitivity to another's suffering, is even more despicable.

Redemptive Suffering

The great Russian philosopher and Orthodox Christian, Nikolai Berdyaev, makes a valid and crucial point when he states that

> in Buddhism, compassion means a desire that the sufferer should attain non-being and is a refusal to bear suffering on behalf of others as well as oneself. In Christianity, compassion means a desire for a new and better life for the sufferer and a willingness to share his pain.

Buddhist compassion is really pity. It does not rise to the level of Christian compassion because it lacks both love in the person who has pity and hope for the other who is suffering. This is why Berdyaev goes on to say that pity may "turn into the worst possible state, into the rejection . . . both of God and man." Pity can be a source of rebellion against God.

For the Christian, suffering is not necessarily meaningless. Indeed, it can be redemptive. For a Christian to share the suffering of another means that, by so doing, he brings a light into the pain and misery of that person's life. He blesses the other person's existence with a higher meaning. Christian compassion is thus bound up with the mystery of the Cross.

Humanistic compassion, another variety of false compassion, is based on the illusion that it is possible to free human beings from suffering altogether and supply them with uninterrupted happiness. This illusion is rampant in the present therapeutic culture, which believes that the road to happiness passes through pharmaceutical companies. But since humanistic compassion is neither realistic nor rooted in love, it is simply another form of pity.

Hoche and Binding, in *The Release of the Destruction of Life Devoid of Value*, a notorious work published in 1920 that paved the way for the Nazi eugenics program, wrote eloquently about "compassion." In one passage, characteristic of their books, the authors write:

> A terrible testimony of the morals of our time! We are spending lots of time, patience, and care on the survival of life devoid of value. Every reasonably thinking person would hope for its end. Our compassion is going beyond a reasonable measure until it reaches cruelty. To deny the incurable patient the peaceful death he so much desires is no longer compassion but the opposite.

Along the spectrum of human dispositions that one can have toward his suffering neighbor, there is pitilessness or insensitivity; Buddhist, humanistic, or other forms of pity; and true compassion that is rooted in love and animated by hope.

A person who experiences pity is in a position to feel morally superior to those who are devoid of pity. And in this case, he is right. But a little bit of rectitude can be a dangerous thing. What he may not realize is the moral superiority of loving compassion. But he very well may, filled with a sense of humanistic righteousness—Jack Kevorkian and Derek Humphry leap to mind—launch a euthanasia program that is nominally compassionate but essentially inhumane. Such is the theme of Rita Marker's penetrating book, *Deadly Compassion*.

Feeling Others' Pain

The problem with pity is not that it is inhumane. It is only too humane. Its problem is that it cannot transcend suffering, finds no meaning in it, and is, in fact, over-whelmed by it. Pity, ultimately, is so humane that it excludes God. Ivan Karamazov, in Dostoevsky's great novel, *The Brothers Karamazov*, could not believe in God as long as one child was in torment. One of Albert Camus' heroes could not accept the divinity of Christ because of the slaughter of the innocents.

The various modes of popular pity mark our gain in sensibility, but at the cost of narrowing our vision to the point where pain is all that we can see. Christianity and the therapeutic culture are at odds with each other on the fundamental question of how we should respond to another's pain. Christianity is by no means insensitive to pain nor to the anguish of the sufferer. But, unlike the therapeutic culture, the Christian brings to his suffering neighbor love, hope, and the light of the Cross.

· COMPASSION II ·

According to Jewish folklore, every baby has a teacher in the womb, an angel who imparts all the world's knowledge. But, at the moment of birth, the same cherub touches the child's lips and takes it all away. "In the mother's body man knows the universe, in birth he forgets it." Thus, we spend our life outside the womb trying to relearn what we originally knew within it.

The Hebrew language indicates that the womb is, indeed, a place of learning, but one where dispositions are acquired which, unlike knowledge, are *not* forgotten. One important and characteristic example is that the Hebrew word for *womb*, *rechem*, is also the root for the word *compassion* or mercy, *rechamim*. The original meaning of compassion, therefore, is the feeling that the mother has for her child or the feeling that siblings born from the same womb have for each other. We find a similar insight in the Egyptian myth of Isis and Osiris, who fell deeply in love with each other while they shared the same womb. The goddess, Isis, came to be regarded as "the mother of all things." This reverential attitude toward the womb, however, has changed in recent years. New reproductive technologies have been an important factor in bringing about this change. As the incubator replaces the womb, the vice of alienation replaces the virtue of compassion.

Womb Anxiety

The well-known and highly influential bioethicist, Joseph Fletcher, who looks upon the womb with deep suspicion, has asked for a ban on all natural childbirth. "The womb is a dark and dangerous place," he writes, "a hazardous environment. We should want our potential children to be where they can be watched and protected as much as possible."

Isaac Asimov concurs, arguing that an embryo developing outside the body can be more easily monitored for birth defects and, eventually, for desirable gene patterns. He also endorses in vitro gestation because it would help women gain an important measure of equality with men. If women could, as he puts it, "extrude the fertilized ovum for development outside the body, she would then be no more the victim of pregnancy than a man is."

Edward Grossman predicts that the time will come when natural pregnancy will become an anachronism and the womb will shrink to appendix-like proportions. At such time, girls can choose to be superovulated at the age of twenty, have their eggs collected and frozen to be thawed and used whenever they decide the time has arrived to start the process of artificially fertilizing and incubating their progeny. On the other hand, others believe that a child who is gestated apart from the warmth of its mother's womb would become "a psychological monstrosity."

Unloving Compassion

Contemporary society has a love affair with the notion of compassion. Not content with using compassion as a mere virtue, it elevates it to the status of an all-embracing moral principle. Hence, it calls upon compassion whenever it wants to resolve a difficult moral problem. We now have divorce, abortion, and, to a certain extent, euthanasia for "compassionate" reasons. The irony has completed its circuit. The virtue that begins in the most deeply physiological and protracted intimacy that exists between two human beings is now routinely summoned to justify their alienation from each other. If society had any real concern for compassion as a virtue, it would be wise to reflect on its roots which, according to various traditions, lies in the uterine intimacy between human beings. To undermine motherhood and the symbolism of the womb is to undermine the wellsprings of compassion.

A Promise

Edwarda O'Bara was a mild diabetic. Around Christmastime in 1969, when she was sixteen, she caught the flu. Then, a few days later on January 3, whether she was prescient or had some premonition of what was about to commence, she said to her mother: "Promise you won't leave me, will you, Mommy?" "Of course, not," replied her mother, "I would never leave you, darling, I promise. And a promise is a promise!"

That was the last conversation Edwarda had with her mother before she slipped into a diabetic coma that has lasted for nearly thirty years. True to her promise, Kaye O'Bara has dutifully, and more important, lovingly cared for her daughter round-the-clock. Except for a few days, Kaye has been with her daughter all the time: feeding her every two hours, testing her blood and giving her insulin injections every four hours, bathing and massaging her, speaking and singing to her, caring for her sundry and persistent needs. She sleeps in a chair, but only in short snatches. Medical bills have been astronomical, and debts have continued to mount.

The account of the relationship between Kaye and her daughter is told simply and respectfully by Dr. Wayne Dyer and his wife, Marcelene. They subtitle their book, *An Almost Unbelievable Story of a Mother's Love and What It Can Teach Us*. The book teaches us about the fruits of unconditional love.

A Mother's Love

Christianity came into the world because a woman, Mary of Nazareth, was willing to make her child the center of her life. What great gifts continue to stream into this world as a result of a mother's love for her child? There are accounts of happenings that are so extraordinary that labeling them as "miracles" seems advisable. There are the reported visitations to Kaye of Mary, the Mother of God, who brings the assurance that one day Edwarda will awaken. There is the lesson that a "victim soul," such as Edwarda's, can bring extraordinary graces into the world and can warm hearts and inspire generosity.

Author Wayne Dyer has been so touched by the O'Baras that he has consigned all the book's royalties to the Edwarda O'Bara fund. His generosity has proven to be eminently salutary since the book has sold more than 50,000 copies.

The love Kaye has shown for her daughter offers us a much-needed image of true compassion. The world needs to know that compassion is not a reason for killing, but an expression of love that unites one with another's suffering.

· MAGNANIMITY ·

Magnanimity, as its etymology indicates, means "greatness of soul." Its definition, however, is much more specific, referring to a person's ability to do great things without being particularly concerned about their consequent honors or applause. According to Saint Thomas Aquinas, "a [magnanimous] man strives to do what is deserving of honor, yet not so as to think much of the honor accorded by man."[1]

As a virtue, magnanimity includes humility, confidence, and hope, but excludes their close neighbors, the vices of presumption, ambition, and vainglory. A magnanimous person must have the humility to know what he can do, the confidence that he can do it, and the hope that his plans will come to fruition. If he overestimates his abilities, he is presumptuous; if he desires to accomplish more than is realistic, he is ambitious; if he exults in his accomplishments, he is vainglorious.

Corrupt Glory

It may be easier to accomplish great works than to be magnanimous in the process. As Aristotle points out:

---

[1] *Summa Theologiae*, IIa IIae, q. 129, art. 1.

For without virtue it is not easy to bear gracefully the goods of fortune; and, being unable to bear them, and thinking themselves superior to others, they despise others and themselves do what they please.[2]

The proud or arrogant man, in attempting to do great things, may bring upon himself great spiritual harm. He may poison his own soul in such a way that it leads to excessive self-absorption as well as contempt for other people. "Beware of the desire for glory," warned Cicero, "for it enslaves the mind." In the process of trying to make great things, a person may unmake himself. Magnanimity, therefore, is the virtue that can prevent a person from corrupting his soul.

A Question of Character

As a youth, Count Henri de Saint-Simon was awakened each morning by his valet who would cry: "Arise, Monsieur le Comte, you have great things to do today." Born in 1760, Saint-Simon was brought up to be conscious of the nobility of his ancestry and the importance of maintaining the luster of his family name. He claimed to have been visited by Charlemagne who predicted that Saint-Simon would become a philosopher of the first rank. Despite this alleged visitation, Saint-Simon did not achieve greatness in any field. In 1823 he was a failed social revolutionary. He was also depressed and utterly destitute. In his despair, he attempted to end his life by shooting himself in the head. He succeeded, however, only in losing an eye. Two years later, at death's door, he gathered his few disciples around him and said, "Remember that in order to do

---

[2] *Ethics*, book 4, section 3.

great things one must be impassioned." Yet he had done nothing to warrant such an operatic ending. Saint-Simon is remembered, as historian Robert Heilbroner points out, far more for his "perversity of character" than for any great achievement.

Carl Maria von Weber, by contrast, accomplished great things while remaining truly magnanimous. The father of the Romantic Movement in music was seriously ill with tuberculosis. His doctor advised him to take a year's rest in Italy, a respite from work that might add five to six years to his life. At the same time, von Weber had been invited to come to London with a new opera that he would conduct with a guaranteed return of $5,000. Work on the opera, according to the doctor, would kill him. Yet von Weber urgently needed to make provision for his wife and children. "As God wills," he said, and set to work on his opera. *Oberon* was greeted with great acclaim and von Weber was the toast of London. But eight weeks after the opera's completion, he died. It was for his music and his family, not for honor, that von Weber engaged in his final labor.

Hold the Applause

Ulysses S. Grant, America's eighteenth president, was a man who accomplished many great things despite his evident absence of ambition. Even his presidency was something he did not seek. "The office has come to me unsought," he stated in his inaugural address.

After his retirement from the White House, Grant and his wife made a world tour, which he had intended to be a private affair. But government officials honored him wherever he went as the most distinguished living American. As historian Julian Hawthorne has written about the tour, "His simplicity and his greatness were at all times and in all places equally apparent, and greatly elevated the foreign estimate of his country."

Toward the end of his life, Grant lost his entire life savings in an ill-advised investment. He spent his last few years providing security for his family by writing his *Memoirs*. At this time, Grant knew he was dying of cancer. Despite his painful condition, he worked assiduously on the project. He died two months after its completion. The *Memoirs*, published by Mark Twain, proved to be an important contribution to the history of the Civil War. Moreover, their modest tone and strength and simplicity of style attest to the magnanimous individual who wrote them. They were immensely successful and secured for Grant's family earnings of approximately $500,000.

For both von Weber and Grant, the praise directed toward their final works was largely posthumous. Yet neither was interested in applause. They were perfect embodiments of what the Duc de la Rochefoucauld once said about magnanimity: "Magnanimity is sufficiently defined by its name; yet we may say of it, that it is the good sense of pride, and the noblest way of acquiring applause."

· BROTHERLY LOVE ·

Scholars do not know the exact date of Christ's birth. It is believed that in the year 354, Pope Liberius decreed that it be celebrated on December 25. He selected this date, in all probability, because the people of Rome already observed it as the Feast of Saturn that celebrated the birthday of the sun. The celebration of the birth of Christ as the Light of the World, therefore, would be in continuity with the pagan celebration of light. Christianity, however, not only carried forward the theme of light, but greatly enriched it with its emphasis on the Star of Bethlehem, glorious choirs of angels, and the Everlasting Light.

Both the Festival of Light and Christmas were preoccupied with extra-terrestrial events. But the perspective was such that man was always looking toward the skies, away from his home on earth. This perspective took a dramatic change thirty years ago when, for the first time, man looked back to earth on Christmas from a position in the heavens.

A New Perspective

On December 21, 1968, a spacecraft appropriately named after the pagan god Apollo left the earth on its three-day trip to the moon. It carried three astronauts: Frank Borman, James A. Lovell, Jr., and William A. Anders. The three were the first human beings to escape from the predominant influence of the earth's gravity, the first to set eyes on the back of the moon, and the first to behold the earth as an object hanging in space.

On December 24, Christmas Eve, the astronauts televised close-up views of the moon as they gazed out their window at planet earth that now seemed no larger than a twenty-five cent piece. The photograph they took of their home planet as they circled the moon has been called the most popular photo of all time, depicting the "blue planet" suspended in space 260,000 miles away, its lower circumference eclipsed by the brim of the moonscape. Lovell spoke of his terrestrial abode as "a grand oasis in the vastness of space."

New Light

As Apollo VIII continued to orbit the moon, the three astronauts took turns reading the biblical account of creation, the first ten verses of *Genesis*. The first voice that could be heard back on earth belonged to William Anders, a Catholic:

> And the earth was without form, and void; and darkness was upon the face of the deep. . . . And God said, Let there be light: and there was light. God saw the light, that it was good: and God divided the light from the darkness.[1]

James Lovell, an Episcopalian, continued: "And God called the light day, and the darkness He called night. And the evening and the morning were the first day. . . ." Frank Borman, also an Episcopalian, then followed:

---

[1] Richard S. Lewis, *Appointment on the Moon* (Binghampton, NY: Vail-Ballou Press, 1969), 455.

And God said let the waters under the heavens be gathered together in one place and the dry land appear: and
it was so. And God called the dry land Earth; and the
gathering together of the waters He called seas: and God
saw that it was good.

And then, on this unique and unprecedented night
before Christmas, Frank Borman, while his spacecraft was
orbiting at ninety miles above the moon's surface, recited a
prayer for all mankind to heed:

Give us, O God, the vision which can see Thy love in the
world in spite of human failure. Give us the faults to trust
Thy goodness in spite of our ignorance and weakness.
Give us the knowledge that we may continue to pray
with understanding hearts, and show us what each one
of us can do to forward the coming of the day of universal peace.

This prayer proved immensely popular in almost every
corner of the world, and among people of diverse faiths as
well as people who were not churchgoers. To many people, its words, transmitted from a spaceship circling the
moon, seemed to be emanating from God Himself. The
following year they were reproduced on countless
Christmas cards.

Peace on Earth
A prayer was sent from space to earth rather than from
earth to space. After returning to earth, Anders stated that

it is quite possible that historians may record that the
greatest gain from Apollo and space exploration, above all
the technical advancements, is this new perspective on
humankind and the earth.

Borman remarked that the astronauts had not begun to realize the magnitude of the positive impact their Christmas message had on people throughout the world until they began reading their mail—as many as 29,000 letters arrived in a single week.

Thirty years ago we had, for the first time, a compelling image of the only home that all we humans can call our own. This image urges us to reflect on the brotherhood, mutual love, and respect that our common dwelling place mandates. The inhospitable blackness of the surrounding void is not an alternative, either literally or figuratively. The perspective had changed. Christmas in 1968 had an earthly, rather than a heavenly, focus. But the enduring message was the same—universal brotherhood and peace to all of goodwill.

· III ·

THE
SOCIAL
VIRTUES

· UNSELFISHNESS ·

The story is told of a Chinese hero who acted with remarkable unselfishness during an earthquake. From the vantage of his hilltop farm, he noticed the ocean swiftly withdraw, like some monstrous animal crouching before a leap. He knew that the leap soon to take place would be a tidal wave. At the same time, he realized that his neighbors, working in the low fields, were in danger of being swept away by the ocean's fury. Without a second thought, he immediately set fire to his own rice ricks and furiously rang the temple bell.

The hero's unselfish act prompted his neighbors to act with similar unselfishness in coming to what they believed to be his aid. The paradox here is that, by acting unselfishly, the neighbors saved their own lives. This paradox is consistent with the Gospel instruction that "[w]hoever seeks to gain his life will lose it, but whoever loses his life will preserve it" (Lk. 17:33).

I vs. We

At the heart of the paradox is the truth of the human being as a *person* and not a mere *individual*. If a human being were merely an individual, unselfishness would be a vice, selfishness a virtue. But a human being is a person whose communal dimension is an inseparable part of his reality. Unselfishness is a virtue because man's destiny is to be whole. And he cannot be whole if he remains a solitary individual.

In her book, *The Virtue of Selfishness*, Ayn Rand makes the mistake of opposing individualism with self-defeating altruism rather than a liberating personalism. She does not understand how self-respect and love for another can be unitary. She does not see the truth of man as a person, that is, one who, in loving, simultaneously affirms both himself and those he loves. Therefore, in her narrow context of individualism, Miss Rand extols "the virtue of *pride*, which is based on the fact that man 'is a being of self-made soul.'"

Communion of Persons

Marriage is a beautiful illustration of how reciprocal unselfishness is expansive and mutually beneficial, not "morally cannibalistic" and "parasitic" (to use Miss Rand's images). In Shakespeare's *King Richard III*, Richard, as Duke of Gloucester, speaks these tender words as he proposes marriage to Lady Anne:

> Look, how this ring encompasseth thy finger,
> Even so thy breast encloseth my poor heart;
> Wear both of them, for both of them are thine.

Why are these words so moving (if we can consider them apart from the rest of the play)? Why do they appear worthy of a future king addressing his queen-to-be? Is it not because they highlight a truth about marriage as a communion of persons?

Cause for Celebration

Husband and wife encircle each other's souls in Holy Matrimony. As they give themselves unselfishly to each other, their souls expand, not contract. Their love for one another allows them to transcend their mere individualities and find a richer existence as two persons in one. This is why marriage is a public celebration, whereas divorce is a private sorrow. People rejoice at the spectacle of a husband and wife enriching their lives as persons by pledging to share them with each other.

Sharing is closed to the strict individualist. Divorce is not the triumphant ascent into individuality. It represents a personal failure, and this is why it is not celebrated. When Adam and Eve impaired their relationship with God, they impaired their relationship with each other. As a result of original sin, they *fell* into individuality. The central meaning of redemption is to recover one's personhood.

The reason that the family, and not the individual, is the basic unit of society is because the family has a program for unselfishness. The individual, by definition, cannot have anything larger than himself as a focus. For this reason, staunch individualists such as Ayn Rand and others denigrate unselfishness. They see it as a threat to the only reality they hold sacred, namely, their own individualities. Individualism, however, can lead only to social anarchy and personal inauthenticity.

More Blessed to Give

Authenticity for the human being means living fully as a *person*. The cult of individuality is a fairly recent notion in the annals of human history. Alexis de Tocqueville remarks in his essay on the French Revolution that the word

> *individualism* was unknown to our ancestors, for the good reason that in their days every individual necessarily belonged to a group and no one could regard himself as an isolated unit.

People do need each other. Economic and cultural deprivations can underscore this mutual need in very dramatic ways. But the virtue of unselfishness is established independently of external conditions. It is a self-forgetful expression of love for others that has the paradoxical effect of enriching the life of the giver.

And the reason it is more blessed to give than to receive is because giving is the most fundamental act of a person. To be a *person* means to give unselfishly. On the other hand, to be an *individual* means to consume, and a life of consumption leads to boredom. "As persons we rule the stars," the saying goes, "as individuals we are ruled by them."

· HUMAN SYMPATHY I ·

Sociologists who believe that their discipline is a science are a distinctively undramatic lot. They believe—religiously, one might say—that black is simply black, and white is nothing other than white. They cannot envision that a man growing up in a dark environment can have a bright future, or that one emerging from a brilliant background can enter into a gray adulthood. Such sociologists know something about social conditioning, but little or nothing about the power of moral virtue and how it can bring drama and optimism into the most sordid and unpromising of lives. They hold the strange belief that it is bad to be monolithic, but wise to be monochromatic. Yet it is at least as narrow and dangerous to be monochromatic as it is to be monolithic. Life is an art whose potentialities are as multiple as the rainbow is colorful.

Hard Times

There was once a young man whose parents, in an attempt to improve the family's finances, purchased a large house that was to be used as a school for young ladies. No pupils ever came, however—not even one. Credit failed. The family's small, well-fingered collection of books was sold. The young man was sent to the pawnbroker with teaspoons, silver teapots, and other small articles that fetched a few shillings. Little by little, the household furniture disappeared, until all that was left was a kitchen table, a few chairs, and the beds. Finally, the father was arrested and placed in debtor's prison.

Our young man, one of eight children born to his improvident and now impecunious parents, was sent to work at a warehouse where he would wrap and label pots of blacking from eight in the morning until eight at night, Monday through Saturday, for six shillings a week. He was barely twelve years old at the time. Living apart from everyone else in his family (and under unbearable conditions), he missed them terribly and visited them in prison every night after work and on Sundays.

He ate bread and milk for breakfast, and his supper consisted of bread and cheese. His lunch was usually stale pastry or a flabby currant pudding. He was not only malnourished, but suffered from painful bouts of colic.

The warehouse itself was a tumbledown building, odorous with dirt and decay. Rats overran its rotted floors and dank cellars. The lad's workmates were coarse and insensitive. They dubbed their out-of-place associate, "the young gentleman." In reflecting on this dark period much later in life, he lamented that he had "no advice, no counsel, no encouragement, no consolation, no support, from anyone that I can call to mind," and added that "but for the mercy of God, I might easily have been, for any care that was taken of me, a little robber or a little vagabond."

Agonizing Lesson

Although his tenure at the blacking warehouse, that produced paste-blacking for boots and fire-grates, was no more than four or five months, the experience seemed an eternity of despair from which he felt no prospect of ever being released. He tearfully expressed to his father that the sun had set on him forever. For posterity, he confided: "No words can express the secret agony of my soul."

But the formative lesson he learned during this period was not despair, but something infinitely more positive. In his study of this extraordinary man, Edgar Johnson states that "the blacking warehouse that made him a man of insuperable resolve and deadly determination, also made him for life a sympathizer with all suffering and with all victims of injustice." In another study of the same man, Norman and Jeanne MacKenzie agree that this dark, seemingly hopeless period "had forged an indissoluble bond of sympathy, even of identity, with the homeless, the friendless, the orphans, the hungry, the uneducated, and even the prisoners of London's lower depths."

His deprivation was so painful that he was determined to become generous. His alienation was so intolerable that he vowed that he would always be sympathetically united with the marginalized. He became one of the world's most successful social revolutionaries. He definitively destroyed, or at least helped to destroy, certain unjust institutions. And he did so with his pen, merely by describing them. G.K. Chesterton could not find a life more paradoxical than his and stated: "If he learnt to whitewash the universe, it was in a blacking factory that he learnt it." Chesterton wrote these words in a book whose title reveals both the identity and the stature of this exceptional human being: *Charles Dickens, The Last of the Great Men*.

Dickens transformed the tribulations that impressed themselves so deeply on him when he was young into the immortal characters he created years later. His father became Mr. Micawber, Mr. Pickwick, or Edward Dorrit; his mother, Mrs. Nickleby; his landlady, Mrs. Pipchin; his first love, Dora Spenlow; and himself, David Copperfield or Oliver Twist.

Dignity for the Poor

His sympathy for all human beings allowed him to spark a social justice revolution without losing sight of the inherent dignity of each person. On the one hand, all his writing seemed to say "Cure poverty"; on the other hand, it was fully in accord with Christ's beatitude, "Blessed are the poor." He was urging improvement in the social conditions of the working class, but at the same time he was showing that the Cratchits, despite their poverty, were still happy, and Scrooge, despite his wealth, was the picture of misery.

Through his novels, Dickens taught that mere pity for the poor is pitiful, but not respectful, and that through loving sympathy we not only unite ourselves with others but help them improve their lives. The truly great man, therefore, is less concerned about his own greatness as he is about the greatness that exists within everyone else. As Chesterton explains, with Charles Dickens in mind, "There is a great man who makes every man feel small. But the real great man is the one who makes every man feel great."

· HUMAN SYMPATHY II ·

"Recommend to your children virtue," Beethoven advised, "that alone can make them happy, not gold." The fact that he had no children of his own does not detract from the legitimacy of these words. Let us consider one man who lived by the spirit of this maxim, Sir Francis Burdett.

In 1820, when an unarmed and orderly crowd of 60,000 men, women, and children were charged by a regiment of cavalry who slashed at them with sabres and trampled them under their horses' hoofs, Sir Francis denounced the authorities who were responsible for the attack, which came to be known as the "Peterloo Massacre." His sharp denunciation, however, resulted in a fine of 2,000 pounds and a sentence of three months in prison. It was not the only time Burdett was imprisoned for expressing his outrage over gross acts of social injustice. But his demonstrations of heroic virtue had a salutary effect on his daughter, Angela, of whom one scholar has stated that "no doubt all her social sympathies were deeply permeated with his influence."

Rich Generosity

Angela Burdett was twenty-three when she became heiress to her grandfather's enormous fortune. It was said that if her capital had been turned into gold-sovereigns, the line would have stretched for twenty-four miles. She lived until the ripe old age of ninety, and all that time never veered from the noble path her father blazed for her to follow. She proved to be entirely capable of managing her great wealth and devoting herself to pious and charitable ends (often anonymously). She founded bishoprics and built churches, supported missionaries, patronized scientists, and encouraged education. Her consistent sympathy for the needs of the oppressed and underprivileged was an essential characteristic of her life. Biographer Edgar Johnson said of her that "she was always to regard her position in society as a responsibility and its use for the welfare of others as a duty."

Baroness Lady Burdett-Coutts, who appended "Coutts" to her surname as a condition of her inheritance from her wealthy grandfather, was widely praised and richly honored. She died on December 30, 1906, approaching her ninety-first birthday. Her body lay in state while a stream of 30,000 mourners filed past. She was buried in Westminster Abbey, where a very close friend of hers who died thirty-six years before her is also buried. At that time, she was the only woman not of royal birth to be so honored.

Partners in Charity

Who was this very close friend, the man she referred to, in fact, as her "complementary self"? And what was the common bond that sustained their relationship for a period of thirty-six years? The friend was none other than Charles Dickens. And the common bond they shared was an abiding sympathy for the downtrodden and a fervent commitment to social justice.

Dickens dedicated *Martin Chuzzlewit* to her, and the glowing praise he offers Mr. Rogers in *The Old Curiosity Shop* could well have been applied to Miss Burdett-Coutts:

[He is] one of the few men whom Riches and Honours have not spoiled and who have preserved in High Places active Sympathy with the Poorest and the Humblest of their kind.

War on Poverty

Charles Dickens wrote more than 500 letters to Angela Burdett-Coutts. Edgar Johnson, who has studied them carefully and includes more than 280 of them in his book, *The Heart of Charles Dickens*, states that their dominate theme refers to the work they were carrying on in the field of social welfare. Concerning Dickens the man, Johnson writes: "[H]ow noble and all-embracing was his demand for social justice."

Dickens carried on his social justice work almost stealthily, fearing that, if his philanthropy were widely known, it would spoil the magic of his books. Therefore, he worked through Miss Burdett-Coutts, as her secretary, as it were, advising how her wealth might best benefit humanity. Together they worked for the abolition of slums, the founding of schools, and the reclaiming of the lives of girls from the streets, honoring the lives of those degraded by poverty. Dickens was anything but an elitist. As he once wrote, "I believe that Virtue shows quite as well in rags and patches as she does in purple and fine linen."

Concerning Dickens the novelist, critical consensus has demonstrated that at the centenary of his death (1970), his standing in English literature is second only to that of William Shakespeare.

In summing up the greatness of Dickens, G.K. Chesterton referred to the novelist's career as his travel, and his life as his joyful association with friends. Thus, he could say that the overriding message that Dickens bequeathed to the world was this: "that comradeship and serious joy are not interludes in our travel; but rather our travels are interludes in comradeship and joy, which through God shall endure forever."

· HOSPITALITY ·

Hospitality, for most of us, is something that belongs to the domain of etiquette. We usually do not think of it as a moral virtue. But when hospitality is animated by a genuine concern for others and is mixed with a generous dollop of social justice, there can be little doubt not only that hospitality can be a moral virtue, but that its embodiment in human behavior can be an inspiration.

Cold Weather, Warm Hearts
Take, for example, the hospitality shown by the town of Grand Forks, British Columbia, during the devastating ice storms in January 1998 that hit Quebec and Eastern Ontario, leaving millions of people without electricity for an extended period of time, in some cases, for several weeks.

Grand Forks is a farming and forestry town located in a valley near the United States border about five hundred kilometers east of Vancouver. Its five thousand residents are not particularly affluent. Unemployment is 11 percent and layoffs are looming in its three wood-processing mills. But generosity is a local tradition.

So, when the citizens of Grand Forks learned about the deprivations their fellow Canadians were experiencing as a result of the century's most damaging ice storm, they were determined to do something to help their suffering neighbors in the East. School Superintendent Denny Kemprud proposed that the town provide hospitality for some students. The idea was met with a wave of enthusiasm, and soon Internet wires were buzzing with plans of adopting seventy-four students, ages thirteen to seventeen, plus four teacher-chaperones to come to Grand Forks.

Air Canada agreed to free up seventy-eight seats. Two hundred families volunteered to provide food and lodging. Grand Forks Secondary School organized committees for transportation, housing, and entertainment. The good citizens of this small community with a big heart chose to rescue their so-called "Eastern refugees" from evacuation centers in hardest-hit Saint-Jean-sur-Richelieu, Quebec.

Gift of Light

When the "refugees" landed at the airport in nearby Kelowna, a local McDonald's restaurant treated them to a free meal before they boarded buses for the ride through the mountains to Grand Forks and their first hot showers in two weeks. The town opened its arms to its guests. The town council presented them with T-shirts. Generous merchants enabled them to go bowling, attend hockey games, and watch the movie *Titanic* at the local theater.

Operation "Freeze Lift" was an immense success. It is a reminder to the world that, with the advent of the Electric Age, we inherit the potential for practicing a new corporal work of mercy: "I was in the dark and you provided me with light." One of the teachers back in Saint-Jean-sur-Richelieu is planning to use the image of hospitality displayed in Grand Forks as a lesson plan for a school course in values, morals, and ethics.

An American author by the name of C.M. Kirkland once said that, "Like many other virtues, hospitality is practiced, in its perfection, by the poor. If the rich did their share, how the woes of this world would be lightened."

East Meets West

Grand Forks, as mentioned, has a tradition of generosity. One-third of its population has descended from Russian Doukhobors or other European immigrants. It hosts summer visits by young radiation patients from Chernobyl and operates a relief program in Russia. When it was time, after two weeks, for the "Eastern refugees" to leave, the Doukhobor church provided them with a mouth-watering feast of Russian fare, including borscht and vereniki dumplings.

Apparently little was mentioned about the political tension between Quebec and the rest of Canada. But if the students harbored any negative feelings about English-speaking Canada, they seemed to have melted under the warmth of Grand Forks hospitality. As one of the teacher-chaperones stated, "The majority of the students will leave here with a different view of the West." One of the students put it this way: "When part of the country is in trouble, that another part would help is something . . . what would you say, strengthening?"

Though somewhat cloistered in the rugged Kootenay Mountains, Grand Forks might appear, to geographical reductionists, as an isolated community. But its strong moral sense of the needs of others gives it a legitimate place on the stage of world affairs. According to philosopher Francis Bacon, "If a man be gracious to strangers, it shows that he is a citizen of the world, and his heart is no island, cut off from other islands, but a continent that joins them."

The residents of Grand Forks, British Columbia, are surely citizens of the world. They are also a moving, albeit modest, example of how morality can be a more powerful factor in unifying people, as well as a nation, than politics.

· CONVIVIALITY ·

Let us begin by making a simple but important distinction between "feeding" and "eating." Horses have feedbags, birds have their bird feeders, and cows feed on grass that grows wild. "Eating," on the other hand, is a specifically human activity. Properly speaking, human beings "eat," rather than "feed." There are plenty of "eateries" for people, but there are no "feederies." "Feeding time" occurs at a zoo. When it is "time to eat," it is time to approach a meal with manners.

"Eating out" involves a certain degree of decorum; "feeding out" would suggest, if it were a legitimate expression, an activity in which decorum would not be expected. Eating is an art form, feeding is a flow. We get much "feedback"; but there is no such thing as "eatback." In German, this difference between *essen* (eating) and *fressen* (feeding) may be even clearer and sharper than it is in English.

Parents understand this difference very deeply, and when they prepare a meal for the family, they expect that it will be an occasion for *eating*, not merely *feeding*.

Filling the Soul

Parents are natural educators who know instinctively that when their children come to the table, they bring with them not only a hunger in the belly, but a hunger in the soul. This latter hunger is for a more spiritual kind of food, but one that easily and naturally accompanies the food which they ingest. There is the hunger for God that is acknowledged in the prayer of thanksgiving, the hunger for community that is satisfied in conversation, the hunger for civility that is appeased in displaying good manners, and the hunger for beauty that is quenched in the decorous setting of the table.

Parents know that humanized, civilized eating can nourish our souls as well as our bodies. Eating can be an experience that rises from a physical necessity to a smorgasbord of spiritual delights. Parents know this in their bones. Unfortunately, they can easily lose sight of it in their day-to-day lives. Moreover, our society, fiercely devoted to convenience, does little to remind them of the singular importance of the family meal and the overflowing richness it represents.

No Time for Togetherness

Ours is the society that has produced the TV dinner, the pizza-and-video supper, fast food that is also *junk* food, paper plates and plastic utensils, and eating on the run as well as eating on the fly. (Thanks to the Concorde, we can now have lunch in New York and indigestion in Paris.) Eating has been reduced to feeding and, in the process, the niceties that help to humanize a meal have quietly evaporated, one by one.

The fast pace of present society challenges those parents who understand that a good meal is nourishment for the hungry soul. But the chief obstacle is the children themselves. They do not seem to know that they come to the table with a hungry soul. For them, the table is a refueling center, a pit stop for the stomach. Therefore, parents must explain, patiently and persistently, that there are more riches to be enjoyed at the table than food for the belly.

The family is not a place where the spiritual anorexia of this age should be fostered.

Furthermore, parents should not lose heart. Society is grievously wrong when it denigrates meal preparation as a demeaning task. Mothers should resist this tenet of feminism. Nor is the father necessarily improving the family meal when he commercializes it by taking everyone out to a restaurant. Man's home should still be his castle. And the father's place in leading the prayers before and after the meal cannot be overestimated.

Family Food

Family meals will often involve mayhem—"Don't eat like a pig, Billy. Stop wolfing down your food!"; "Sit up straight, Lisa, and stop poking your brother!" "No, you can't leave the table just yet, Sarah," and so on *ad infinitum*. But parents should not cave in. Education of the sensibilities is always slow and arduous. The family meal cannot be abandoned or compromised. Too many personal and communal values are at stake.

There are two fundamental rituals that are indispensable for solidifying family unity. One is going to church together and praying as a family. The other is eating a meal together in a way that instills conviviality, a priceless virtue embracing gratitude, generosity, appreciation, physical and spiritual delectation, comradery, cooperation, and love. The family meal is worth all the effort and countless frustrations that inevitably accompany it. There are simply no adequate substitutes for it.

There was a meal our eldest ancestors shared in which they purposely excluded God. Perhaps by partaking of the forbidden fruit in this manner, they reduced eating to feeding. We cannot imagine them saying grace before their meal. At any rate, we do know that they fell from grace and suffered acutely from a kind of psychic indigestion, which they passed on, in some degree, to all of us. A good family meal, on the other hand, can be like an experience of eternity, for, as the Italians say (and we have reason to believe that they know something about the importance of good family meals): "A *tavola non s'invecchia*" (At the table one never grows old).

· FAIRNESS ·

The difference between fairness and justice, though subtle, is pivotal in the area of virtue education. A firm grasp of fairness is needed before one can gain a proper appreciation of the value of justice.

No Fairness in Bible?

Sacred Scripture offers us little help in making this distinction. "Fairness" does not appear in the Bible. The term "fair" appears many times, though usually without a moral meaning. For the most part, it describes someone or something that is comely, beautiful, well-constructed, or placid. In Job 42:15, we read, "[T]here were no women so fair as Job's daughters." In Song of Songs 6:10, the bride is praised as being "fair as the moon, bright as the sun." In Numbers 24:5, the author exclaims, "How fair are your tents, O Jacob!" In Acts 27:8, Saint Paul arrives at a safe port on the southern coast of Crete that is named Fair Havens.

There is but one exception to the non-moral use of the word "fair." In Matthew 15:26 and Mark 7:27, Christ tells the Canaanite woman: "It is not fair to take the children's bread and throw it to the dogs." The Greek word employed in both these texts is *kalóv*, which is sometimes translated as "right" rather than "fair." *Kalóv* is a versatile word and can also describe that which is beautiful, good, or proper. Yet "fair" in these two passages is not distinguishable from "right" or "just."

Child's Play

How is being fair different from being just? And why is this difference important? Fairness differs from justice in three important ways. It is broader, more elementary, and less formal than justice.

Fairness has a much broader range of applicability than justice. It can refer to the beautiful (*My Fair Lady*), the civil (fair words), the good (a fair crop), or the unobstructed (the fairway). In meteorology, it distinguishes fair from bad weather; in baseball, a fair from a foul ball; in business, a fair shake from a shady deal; and in law, a fair trial from a kangaroo court. The utility of fairness is extensive because it is an easier concept to grasp than justice. It applies to the cosmos as well as to children at play.

The fact that youngsters use the word "fair" long before they employ the word "just" is a good indication that the concept of fairness is more elementary than that of justice. It may very well be that the first moral judgment a child utters is "That's not fair!" Virtually all studies on the subject report that children as young as four already have an active and flourishing sense of fairness. Accompanying their strong sense of fairness is their intense disdain for cheating, cutting in line, grabbing more than one's share, and taking unfair advantage of others.

Justice can be highly complex and legalistic. It lends itself quite naturally to being institutionalized. Lawyers, judges, and other professionals who defend and uphold the law require a great deal of training. Fairness, by contrast, is not nearly as formal. In fact, a sense of fairness seems to be quite spontaneous and natural. The unschooled can easily appreciate the need for fairness. On the other hand, one who is highly educated in the field of jurisprudence may lose sight of fairness' basic value.

Justice Comes Later

These three characteristics—broader, more elementary, less formal—give fairness certain practical advantages over justice in the area of virtue education. Since children have such a natural and keen appreciation for fairness, it would seem reasonable to affirm and cultivate that sense in them as much as possible. In so doing, children would be better prepared to develop a richer understanding and appreciation for justice. Just as the broad comes before the specific, the elementary anticipates the complex, and the informal is prior to the formal, a sense of fairness precedes a sense of justice.

In practice, adults can help young people to cultivate a sharper sense of justice not only by honoring their sense of fairness, but especially by being good examples of fairness themselves. We speak of a chief justice or a justice of the peace, but we do not speak of a chief fairness or a fairness of the peace. There is something innocent and down-to-earth about the language of fairness. It does not need professionals or manuals. It appeals to people's innate sense of sociability and their admirable willingness to temper self-interest for the sake of friendship.

Even Steven

Two economists, Elizabeth Hoffman and Matthew Spitzer, gave pairs of college students an intriguing choice. By the flip of a coin, one member of the pair would win the privilege of choosing either to receive twelve dollars (while his partner would receive nothing) or fourteen dollars, provided he and his partner agreed in advance how they would split the larger sum. The economists found that fairness, rather than self-interest, prevailed. Most students decided in advance that they would split the fourteen dollars evenly. They obviously believed that a flip of a coin was not a fair way of allocating unequal benefits. At the same time, this preference for fairness does much to affirm amicability. The choice to be fair is also a choice not to allow self-interest to compromise sociability.

If justice has to do with law, fairness has to do with the heart. Members of a family can be fair to each other without ever having recourse to the language of justice. But those who are well-schooled in the informal art of fairness will make excellent candidates for the more formal art of justice.

· JUSTICE ·

We usually think of justice in relation to our dealings with other people. Justice requires us to render each person his due. Most of us understand justice, therefore, as a personal or social virtue.

Being just to other people, however, presupposes a more fundamental order of justice in which we name things justly. We could not fulfill our obligation in justice to pay another the ten dollars we owe him if we fail to call a sawbuck a sawbuck, and instead call it ten cents. As Saint Augustine writes, "Whatever is against truth cannot be just." To be just to another person rests on our initially being just to the truth. Personal justice is based on philosophical justice.

You Be the Judge

Our understanding not only of justice but also of virtue in general is greatly impaired when we mislabel vice as virtue, and virtue as vice. Calling fair foul, as Shakespeare suggests, is a devilish enterprise. If the word is wrong, then the thought is wrong. And if the thought is wrong, then the resulting action is wrong. The correct naming of things is indispensable to correct thinking and correct acting. Before justice exists in action, it must first exist in word and thought.

There is a scene in Sir Walter Scott's novel *Anne of Geierstein* that eloquently and dramatically brings to light the insidious and unjust practice of calling vice virtue.

In the story, the brave young Arthur is riding in the company of Thiebault. The latter, a grandson of troubadours and a lover of ballads, sings one with great artistry for his traveling companion.

The ballad unfolds a rather sordid saga. A certain troubadour by the name of William Cabestaing is in love with Margaret, the wife of Baron Raymond de Roussillon. When the husband learns of the affair, he kills Cabestaing, cuts out his heart, and has it cooked like an animal's. He then serves it to his wife, but does not reveal its nature until after she has finished eating it. Margaret's response to this ghastly deed is stoic and sacrificial. She quietly explains that the food was so precious to her that her lips "should never touch coarser nourishment." She persists in her macabre decision and starves herself to death.

The ballad goes on to weave the rest of the story:

> Every bold knight in the south of France assembled to besiege the baron's castle, stormed it by main force, left not one stone upon another, and put the tyrant to an ignominious death.

It is clear by his manner that Thiebault approves of Margaret's suicide and the vengeance heaped upon her husband.

Finding the Right Words

Arthur takes a decidedly different view of the matter. He admonishes his companion:

> Thiebault, sing me no more such lays. I have heard my father say that the readiest mode to corrupt a Christian man is to bestow upon vice the pity and the praise which are due only to virtue. Your Baron of Roussillon is a mon-

ster of cruelty; but your unfortunate lovers were not the less guilty. It is giving fair names to foul actions that those who would start at real vice are led to practice its lessons, under the disguise of virtue.

Sir Walter Scott has his bold hero, Arthur, speak like a saint or Father of the Church. It is not just, Arthur is saying, to call vice by the name of virtue. But not only that, such philosophical injustice—a kind of injustice to being— inevitably leads to the practice of real vice. Philosophical injustice breeds personal and social injustice.

Arthur's advice is timeless. We could use a novelist of the moral acumen of Sir Walter Scott in our own time. Consider the current penchant for giving vice fair words: Vengeance is getting even, pornography is adult entertainment, sterilization is a way of getting fixed, abortion is merely a choice, and euthanasia is an act that is replete with dignity.

Pope John Paul II affirms that when our consciences can call "evil good and good evil" (Is. 5:20), we are "already on the path to the most alarming corruption and the darkest moral blindness."[1]

Nice Guys Finish Last

Not long ago, a particularly hard-headed business woman graced the cover of *Fortune* magazine. The following words ran alongside the image of her gritty and determined countenance: "The toughest Babe in Business—Darla Moore married Richard Rainwater, tripled his wealth, axed Boone

---

[1] Pope John Paul II, Encyclical Letter On The Gospel of Life *Evangelium Vitae*, no. 24.

Pickens, and pushed Rick Scott out at Columbia/HCA. Stay Tuned." The message is only too clear: If you want to get ahead, and receive the enviable plaudits of *Fortune* magazine, you had better be tough.

The business world finds it easy to praise heartlessness as being tough. Being just is not likely to catapult a fair-minded entrepreneur to the cover of a major success magazine. Nice guys, presumably, finish last.

Philosophical justice—naming things rightly in accord with what they are—is indeed a virtue. It is as delicate, however, as it is fundamental. And this is precisely why it must be taken seriously. It is easy to ignore or distort philosophical justice, while urging people to preach social justice from the housetops. But the truth is that there can be no social justice without giving vice its due by calling it vice, and without singing the praises of virtue for the plain fact that it is virtuous.

· SOCIAL JUSTICE ·

The expression "social justice" has been particularly well marketed. Everyone, it seems, is a champion of social justice. Groups may disagree with each other on nearly every moral issue but, when it comes to social justice, they all stand up and salute.

It is only too clear that social justice means different things to different people. One essential point that distinguishes the Catholic Church's notion of social justice from its secular counterpart has to do with the concept of personal virtue. The Church's great social encyclicals, from Leo XIII's *Rerum Novarum* to John Paul II's *Centesimus Annus*, emphasize again and again that there can be no separation of social justice from personal virtue, as there can be no divorce between the sphere of social responsibility and that of personal responsibility.

The secular world compartmentalizes the personal and the social, holding that what one does in his personal life—whether as a private citizen or as the president of a nation—has little or no relevance to what he does on a social level. The Church understands social justice as a continuity of the personal and the social, the secular world does not.

Getting Personal

"I am personally opposed, but cannot impose my private values on the public" is a catch phrase that appears only too often on the lips of a secular politician. The truth about anything, however, is not the kind of thing that literally imposes itself. The Second Vatican Council has put the matter this way: "The truth cannot impose itself except by virtue of its own truth, as it wins over the mind with both gentleness and power."[1]

The Church maintains that, in order to have social justice, we must first have virtuous people. The secular world maintains that social justice does not require virtuous people, only good programs. For the Church, social justice is a personal virtue; for the secular world, it is a political accomplishment. The Church believes that good people make good social programs; the secular world believes that good social programs make good people. Concerning social justice, the Church and the secular world have very little in common.

Ethics Without Virtue

Philosophy professor Christina Sommers provides an illuminating as well as amusing example of the folly of waiting for good programs before one can be a good person. She relates an incident involving a colleague who adamantly held that social justice had nothing to do with personal virtue. The colleague said to her: "You are not going to have moral people until you have moral institutions. You will not have moral citizens until you have moral government." She emphasized her point by berating Professor Sommers for wasting her time and even harming her students by promoting bourgeois morality and bourgeois virtues instead of

---

[1] Vatican II, Declaration on Religious Liberty *Dignitatis Humanae* (1965), no. 1, as reproduced in Austin Flannery, O.P., ed., *Vatican II: The Conciliar and Post Conciliar Documents* (Northport, NY: Costello Publishing Co., 1975).

getting them to do something about the oppression of women, corruption in big business, and the evil of multinational corporations.

But a curious thing happened at the end of the semester. More than half of this colleague's students cheated on their social justice take-home exams. "What are you going to do?" Professor Sommers asked her distraught associate. "I'd like to borrow a copy of that article you wrote on ethics without virtue," she replied, with a self-mocking smile.

There is no ethics without virtue any more than the combustion engine operates without fuel or sailboats are driven without wind. Without personal virtue there can be social reform through legislation, power, and coercion, but such impersonal and unvirtuous acts do not produce a condition of social justice in the truest sense of the term. There is no social justice without a civil society, and a civil society cannot exist without personal virtue. Getting good marks on a social justice examination by plagiarizing hardly makes the student a more ethical person.

Gift of Self

Consider an example illustrating an approach that is consistent with Church teaching. On February 26, 1997, members of Christendom College in Front Royal, Virginia, raised $1,107.40 for a local pregnancy center by donating blood. In all, fifty-six people, representing faculty, staff, and student body, gave blood. The number of participants that day was particularly substantial for the relatively small, liberal arts college; one student had to wait four hours before he could finally make his contribution.

There can be little doubt that this collective act of giving blood is an act of social justice. And a particularly instructive one as well, inasmuch as the unselfishness

implied by giving blood, together with the additional significance of transferring blood from one person to another,
beautifully illustrates how generously and profoundly people
can participate in each other's lives as they work together
for the common good.

We must be both the benefactors and the agents of
social justice. By severing personal virtue from social
reform, we hope for the impossible: to reap the harvest of a
crop that was never planted.

· SOLIDARITY I ·

The term "solidarity" is so strongly identified with the Solidarity Movement in Poland, which toppled the Communist government in 1989, that many people naturally assume it is a political force rather than a moral virtue. The truth of the matter is that solidarity is a moral virtue. Moreover, Poland's Solidarity Movement itself is moral. In fact, its virtuous basis was shaped and sustained to a significant extent by the moral philosophy of Karol Wojtyla, the man who would later become Pope John Paul II.

In his most important philosophical work, *The Acting Person* (*Osoba i Czyn*), which won him an honorary doctorate from Harvard University, Wojtyla provides what may very well be the most concise and penetrating treatment of the virtue of solidarity that has ever been penned.

Everything he writes in *The Acting Person* concerning solidarity flows from his understanding of "participation." By this term, Wojtyla refers to the fact that human beings are not confined by their individualities, as atheistic philosopher Jean-Paul Sartre suggests, but rather share in a profound way with the humanity of others. In addition, human beings are able to grasp universal values, such as truth, justice, rights, and peace, which they need in order to become fulfilled.

More Than Politics

Wojtyla develops the notion that solidarity is simply the virtue of care as extended to all other people in society. It involves responsible care for the common good, the moral well-being of the human community. Because solidarity is a virtue, it springs from a heart of love. This is, in essence, what distinguishes it from a political reality. Politics participates in a process; solidarity, more spiritual in nature, participates in humanity.

Family members, let us say, care for each other, and their mutual love is palpably present in that form of care. The care that members of society have for each other precisely as members of society is the substance of solidarity. In this instance, however, love may not be immediately recognized as love, since it may lack specific emotional intensity and its benefactors and beneficiaries may be strangers to each other.

Wojtyla makes it clear that love is indeed at the heart of solidarity when he insists that we should recognize members of society as "neighbors." Our relationship with our neighbor should be one of love, for love is the only appropriate attitude one should have for another person. Thus, the fittingness of Christ's commandment to love our neighbor as ourself. To be sure, "neighbor" and "member of the community" overlap, just as do personal love and civic responsibility. But the primacy of love for neighbor gives solidarity an interior depth that is lacking in purely civic or political attitudes. Solidarity has a political goal, but it has a personal—and therefore virtuous— essence. The commitment to love is, in fact, a call to experience another human being as another self, that is, to participate in another's humanity.

Virtue of Virtues

Solidarity, as the virtue that extends care to one's neighbors, will not remain serviceable unless it is allied with several other virtues. In *The Acting Person*, Wojtyla points out how solidarity and opposition go hand in hand. Without opposition, solidarity degenerates into conformism. On the other hand, opposition without solidarity collapses into noninvolvement. Hence, it is imperative that virtues of courage, discernment, patience, and open-mindedness be cultivated. These virtues serve the need to dialogue with one's opposition.

General Wojciech Jaruzelski, who, as Communist Poland's president, was the most powerful opponent to the Solidarity Movement, confesses how much he was impressed by Pope John Paul II's ability to engage in respectful dialogue. The Holy Father, as Jaruzelski attests,

> is a man who knows how to listen calmly even when he disagrees completely with what he hears. . . . This touched me very much. . . . Every meeting I have had with him brought us closer together in a purely human sense—not only in an intellectual format, but with warmth.

Must Be True!

Wojtyla is careful to note that dialogue, if it is to be authentic, must take place within the context of truth. Moreover, members of any solidarity group will work with each other for the common good most effectively when they honor each other's complementary gifts. Therefore, a spirit of mutual understanding and cooperation among the members is necessary.

Sociologist Dennis Wrong writes:

> Solidarity based on shared norms, commitment to col-
> lective goals, and the maintenance of a system of dif-
> ferentiated roles, are defining criteria of all stable
> groups, including groups whose *raison d'etre* [reason for
> existence] may be in conflict with other groups.[1]

In this statement, Professor Wrong reiterates many of the
points that are common to Wojtyla's concept of solidarity:
the common good, the notion of a community, the need for
complementarity, and the importance of opposition and
dialogue. Wrong's understanding of solidarity, however,
remains merely political because it lacks two vital elements
that are essential to Wojtyla's notion of participation—
namely, love of neighbor and desire for truth. It is precisely
these two elements—rooted in the dignity and transcen-
dence of the human person—that identify Wojtyla's notion
of solidarity as a truly moral virtue.

---

[1] Dennis Wrong, *The Problem of Order: What Unites and Divides Society*
(New York: The Free Press, 1994).

· SOLIDARITY II ·

The *Acting Person* is Karol Wojtyla's philosophical *magnum opus*. Though it established him as a world-class philosopher and won him an honorary doctorate from Harvard University, it has the not entirely unjustified reputation for being exceedingly difficult to read and comprehend. While he was Bishop of Krakow, his own priests joked that, if one of them was sentenced to purgatory, he would, upon reading the entire text, immediately be sprung into paradise.

At the same time, setting engaging anecdotes aside, *The Acting Person* provided a sufficiently clear and inspiring treatment of the virtue of *solidarnosc* (solidarity) that it was a major factor in shaping and sustaining Poland's Solidarity Movement. In fact, as philosopher Rocco Buttiglione, a close friend of Pope John Paul II, has stated, many of the ideas expressed in *The Acting Person*, particularly those concerning solidarity, actually became popular among the people of Poland.

There are two points of fundamental importance that should be made concerning Wojtyla's contribution to the notion of *solidarnosc*. The first is that what he means by the term is not, in essence, something political. It is only too clear, from his other writings and addresses, that solidarity is a personal and moral virtue rooted in love. The second point is that *solidarnosc* is not exclusively Polish. It is not limited to national significance, but is truly universal in its implication. *Solidarnosc*, then, is loving in its essence and universal in its scope.

Not a Cult

In his introduction to the third Polish edition of *The Acting Person*, Rocco Buttiglione explains that

> solidarity is the attitude of responsible care for the common good which constitutes the human community, or, in other words, the social form of love understood as the sole adequate attitude toward the person.

The fact that the Solidarity Movement in Poland had a personalist depth and a virtuous basis was not immediately evident to its opposing forces. Poland's Communist officials, initially and for some time thereafter, misinterpreted Solidarity as a purely political movement whose masses could not possibly function without their charismatic leader, Lech Walesa. Russian Prime Minister Yuri Andropov spoke derisively about the "cult of Walesa."

Solidarity, however, not only survived repeated acts of political repression and military assault (even during the eleven months in which Walesa was incarcerated), but grew stronger in the process. Members of Solidarity demonstrated the astonishing ability to generate a political system apart from the state. This could not have been accomplished without a strong basis in moral virtue.

On August 31, 1980, the Polish government agreed to recognize labor unions. That year Lech Walesa, an electrician at the Gdansk shipyard, founded Solidarity. On March 19, 1981, two hundred policemen forcibly evicted Solidarity members from a provincial assembly hall for no apparent reason. According to reports, the Solidarity members were beaten; three were hospitalized, including the leader of the local chapter, Jan Rulewski.

On December 12, 1981, Solidarity leaders proposed holding a national referendum on setting up a non-Communist government. The very next day, Communist Party first secretary and Council of Ministers chairman, General Wojchiech Jaruzelski, declared martial law and arrested and confined Solidarity leaders and supporters. According to his own figures, 10,554 people were arrested or confined. On October 8, 1982, Poland's parliament (Sejm) declared Solidarity illegal. Five days later, the government militarized the Gdansk shipyard, drafting the workers into the armed services.

Events such as these made it increasingly clear to more and more people of the world that, in the struggle between Solidarity and the Communist government, it was the former that appeared to be decidedly more democratic and incomparably more committed to universal values such as social justice, human rights, and peace. It was the last value that especially caught the attention of the Nobel Prize committee. In awarding the Nobel Peace Prize to Lech Walesa on October 5, 1983, it called attention to his "contribution, made with considerable personal sacrifice, to insure the workers' right to establish their own organizations" in Poland. It also praised Walesa's determination to avoid violence, and noted that it has "on several occasions, when awarding the Peace Prize, stressed that a campaign for human rights is a campaign for peace."

Spiritual Strength

Karol Wojtyla, as Bishop of Krakow and author of *The Acting Person*, did much to clarify and strengthen the moral and universal quality of Solidarity. As occupant of the

Chair of Peter, he could bring to the consciousness of the world the truth that Solidarity is not merely a Polish political process, a narrowly national movement, but a struggle for justice and human rights that should instruct and inspire people of all nations. Even a year before Solidarity was established in Poland, Pope John Paul II was urging people to understand that for Solidarity to be effective, it must have a moral basis and a universal scope. In Washington, DC, on October 26, 1979, in an address outside the Organization of American States building, he spoke thus:

> The words that are most filled with meaning for man—words such as justice, peace, development, solidarity, rights—are sometimes belittled as a result of systematic suspicion or party and sectarian ideological censure. Then they lose their power to mobilize and attract. They will recover it only if respect for the human person and commitment to the human person are explicitly brought back to the center of all considerations.

The multiplicity of virtues needed in order to sustain Solidarity in the practical realm attests to its personalist basis. A person is morally effective in direct proportion to the number of cultivated virtues he possesses. We may regard the sum total of a person's virtues as forming his *character*. The recent history of Poland's Solidarity Movement is a lesson in character. Poland is the first country to achieve the spiritual strength needed to break free of Communist oppression. Its example served to inspire other democratic movements in other nations to develop a similar spiritual and political freedom. The character displayed by Lech Walesa and Pope John Paul II are encouraging examples of how character can be more practical than force in the quest for peace.

· LEADERSHIP ·

A leadership vacuum exists in our culture. Most people who have thought seriously about the matter agree. Moreover, this is not a matter for mere casual observation, but one that elicits a strong sense of deprivation. We need leaders, and they are as cherished as they are rare.

What are the qualities of a leader? For Aristotle there were three: *ethos*, *pathos*, and *logos*. The *ethos* is his moral character and the source of his ability to convince others; the *pathos* is his ability to touch feelings and move people emotionally; the *logos* is his ability to give solid reasons for particular actions and, therefore, to move people intellectually. By this definition, Socrates, Jesus Christ, Gandhi, Winston Churchill, and Abraham Lincoln were great leaders.

Who's at the Wheel?

What has taken place in the modern world that has created the current absence of great leaders? One factor is the dissociation of leadership from genuine authority, that is, authority that is rooted in truth. In *Between Past and Future*, Hannah Arendt describes how the old authority was lost in the modern world. She deems this loss as "tantamount to the loss of the groundwork of the world." Ever since, she writes, the world "has begun to shift, to change and transform itself with ever increasing rapidity from one shape into another. . . . Everything at any moment becomes almost anything else."[1] We are uprooted. Change is omnipresent and has separated us from anything stable and enduring, including a basis of authority from which a great leader could emerge.

Novelist John Updike has expressed the same predicament in more poetic and arresting terms:

> [We now live in] one of those dark ages that visits mankind between millennia, between the death and rebirth of gods, when there is nothing to steer by but sex and stoicism and the stars.

Needless to say, sex, stoicism, and the stars do not provide a reliable basis for leadership. Those who regard them as holding all the answers to the meaning of life will inevitably mislead and betray their followers. Hugh Hefner (*Playboy*), Jim Jones (The People's Temple), and Marshall Applewhite (Heaven's Gate) are not leaders in the true sense. Both their inspiration and their charismatic appeal derive more from desperation and superstition than from a source that is solid, authoritative, and realistic.

True leadership must be anchored in authority. This is what saves leadership from demagoguery and dictatorship. It is what distinguishes the leader from the false prophet or the self-serving manipulator. Attila the Hun, Genghis Khan, Alexander the Great, Napoleon, and Hitler were conquerors rather than true leaders. Today, authority itself is in a state of crisis.

---

[1] Hannah Arendt, *Between Past and Future* (New York: Penguin Books, 1978), 95.

True Authority

People are commonly suspicious of authority largely for two reasons: they mistake it for something they fear or they fear that it endangers something they love. Thus, they confuse authority with power, and fear that it will rob them of freedom.

Authority is not the same as "authoritarianism." It is neither mere power nor a curtailment of freedom. In fact, the authority of some exists for the liberty of others. Authority, insofar as it is connected with reality, is essentially trustworthy. A person is an authority on birds, for example, because he knows a great deal about them. A person is properly in a position of authority because he is qualified for it. A person has true moral authority if his sense of moral values reflects what is truly good for mankind. All authority ultimately is derived from God. This also explains why a climate of atheism is not conducive to producing great leaders.

Authority is connected with truth. Leadership involves an association with people. Consequently, a leader must have a certain amount of such intangible qualities as zeal, fervor, charm, and charisma. But if the leader has no involvement with truth, he has no substance to offer those who follow him. Those who denigrate parental authority while admiring the exploits of world conquerors do not have much appreciation for what the virtue of leadership entails.

Everyday Heroes

Our present conception of a true leader is just as confused as our notion of authority. In the world of politics, a leader is usually a follower, that is to say, one who learns what people want and promises to give it to them if they will elect him to office. In the world of sports, a leader is understood to be a front-runner, one who puts some distance between himself and his competitors.

A true leader, the one for whom a culture has such great need, is neither an opportunistic follower nor an ambitious front-runner. If he is truly to lead people to some fulfilling destiny, as Moses did, he must lead them without separating himself from them. He must be uncommon enough to inspire people to struggle to achieve a good end. At the same time, he must be common enough so that the common man can emulate him. The paradox of the uncommon-common man is also the paradox of the servant leader. Pope Gregory the Great referred to himself as the "servant of the servants of God" ("*Servus servorum Dei*"). Pope John Paul II sees his own leadership in accordance with this same paradigm. A father's leadership follows the same form.

The Right Stuff

We desire leaders, yet we cut their legs out from under them when we distrust authority and separate leadership from real moral values. We then settle for a variety of pseudo-leaders: the celebrity, the cult leader, the vote-getter, the front-runner, the overachiever, and the trend-setter. But true leadership rarely emerges from political, economic, or cultural forces. It is the consequence, for the most part, of religious and spiritual potentialities.

Socrates, Jesus, Gandhi, Lincoln, and Pope John Paul II were and are great leaders who emerged from extremely humble origins. But none of them were at all undernourished spiritually.

The problem of leadership, complex as it is, has a correlative problem in the problem of "followership." Part of the wisdom needed to recognize a true leader is the wisdom to know how to be a good follower. If we are to make our own exodus from bondage, we must be able to recognize not only who Moses is, but who he is not. And Moses, we must remember, could lead only because he knew whom to follow. God is our leader in the truest sense; all other leaders follow in His light.

· HONOR ·

President William Jefferson Clinton signed a proclamation in 1996 during National Character Week which read:

> [I]ndividual character involves honoring and embracing core ethical values: honesty, respect, responsibility. . . . Parents must teach their children from the earliest age the difference between right and wrong. But we must all do our part.

In retrospect, in the aftermath of the Clinton/Lewinsky imbroglio, one might say that never before has an American statesman more insincerely set his signature to a public document. The bright side of hypocrisy, of course, is the tribute it pays to virtue. If one does not honor core moral values in practice, at least he can honor them on parchment. Honor, then, is not entirely dead. It just needs cardiopulmonary resuscitation.

Don't Mention It
The Associated Press published its list of All-American basketball players recently. A sizeable group of athletes who did not make the First, Second, or Third Teams, made "Honorable Mention." These players, who worked hard and performed admirably on the basketball court, were *honored* in this way, an honor they no doubt cherish. Not to have honored them, in the minds of hoop aficionados, would be unthinkable, an unforgivable dereliction of duty. High

performance on the hardwood must be honored. That is not optional. Honoring people for high moral performance in life *is* optional, if not counterproductive, since it might wound the self-esteem of those who are not so honored.

In his address to the U.S. Naval Academy entitled "Does Honor Have a Future?" William J. Bennett asked the question:

> If the character and personal conduct of the acknowledged leader of the free world is "irrelevant," then what is relevant? Why should anyone feel compelled to make sacrifice for the sake of an abstract principle of honor?

To Die For

By defining honor as "abstract," Bennett's question contains a clue to its own answer. Honor is abstract only to the man who is dishonorable. Honor does not have a future among the dishonorable. But the honorable person sees honor as flowing from that which is most sacred in himself. Honor, like love and intelligence, is one of the most concrete of all human realities. The honorable person would no more abandon his honor than abandon his parents, turn against his friends, or betray his country. Honor is the resonance, the electricity, if you will, that vibrates between two souls. Husbands and wives honor each other as a way of affirming and co-celebrating the real values they see in each other. To the honorable, honor is not an abstract principle. It is the natural and spontaneous way that they show how much they cherish that which is sacred. "The sublimest absurdity," as Martin Buber has reminded us, "is to throw away that which is most precious in yourself."

The problem is not how to honor what is honorable, but how people can become honorable. The problem is concrete, not abstract. People take their first steps toward becoming honorable when they recognize beyond the shadow of a doubt that there is something in the universe far more glorious than themselves—something, indeed, that might even be worth dying for.

G.K. Chesterton, in his remarkably insightful book, *What's Wrong With the World?* makes the statement that "[i]n everything on this earth that is worth doing, there is a stage when no one would do it, except for necessity or honor." There are moments of tedium in anything that is worth doing, and they must be survived out of necessity or honor if we are to continue along the right path. We survive the moments of doubt or difficulty in our marriage or career or even a basketball contest not through pleasure of convenience, but through honor. Honor glues us to our task when none of the ordinary creature comforts are there to sustain us. Honor is the noble and self-effacing commitment to do what is honorable because it is honorable—not because it is personally gratifying. Honor is the purity of one's pledge to do what is right. It is the crown of unselfishness, the generosity of the soul, and the recognition that there are objective values loftier than egoism.

The Roman naturalist, Pliny the Elder, wrote: "Let honor be to us as strong an obligation as necessity is to others." That one's word can be his bond indicates great strength of will. It is surely a noble and honorable soul that finds honor as compelling as necessity, who does not regard dishonor as being an option. We say that such a person has integrity, integrity so durable and reliable that it will not be fractionalized by self-interest. Such a person is indeed rich because his bond to everything in the cosmos that is good and holy enlarges him.

In order to become honorable one must first become a *person*. The mere *individual* sees only himself, and consequently he finds honor to be abstract and contrary to self-interest. But the *person*, that is, the one who combines the uniqueness of his individuality with the communal dimension of his personality, will find honor to be the natural way in which he defends and protects, reveres and esteems those goods that are worth loving.

· IV ·

THE
SACRED
VIRTUES

· OBEDIENCE ·

Obedience, to the secular mind—and more so than any other virtue—seems to be a vice. This is because the secular world prizes individual freedom above all else, and can see nothing in obedience but the renunciation of that freedom, together with servile submission to the will of another. As the philosopher Jean-Jacques Rousseau has advised, no one person should have authority over another person—we should obey only ourselves.

By the same token, there is no more certain route to personal disaster than obeying only oneself. We are not so wise or self-sufficient that we can afford to shut our minds to all others and find our way through life solely by listening to and obeying ourselves. How many of us can say that he even *knows* himself? Yet, if an individual presumes to be self-sufficient, why should he not expect to exercise his authority over others? Moreover, would a society of closed and self-sufficient individuals be able to cooperate with each other? Or would they engage in rancorous and incessant feuds with one another to the detriment of civility and social cohesion? Obeying only oneself is a formula for both alienation as well as anarchy.

I'll Do It My Way

Martin Buber has a more insightful view of the human being. As a mere "I," according to the author of *I-Thou*, the individual becomes hopelessly entangled in the unreal. "He has in truth no destiny," writes Buber, "but only a being that is defined by things and instincts, which he fulfills with the feeling of sovereignty—that is, in the arbitrariness of self-will." The individual who obeys only himself is unable to sacrifice his unfree will—one that is held in bondage to things—to his grand will, which is in harmony with man, society, God, and truth.

Those who see obedience as a vice really see nothing as a virtue. And, if there is nothing that is truly virtuous, one might as well listen only to his own voice. But there is a world of meaning, authority, and virtue. Self-sufficiency is an illusion. And this is why obedience can be a virtue.

Like any other virtue, obedience must be regulated by prudence. No virtue—obedience, courage, generosity, or anything else—is virtuous without prudence, which is the virtue of being realistic. One should not obey himself in all matters, no more than one should obey his horoscope, his enemy, or a manipulator. Obedience needs prudence in order to be virtuous, just as a student needs a teacher in order to learn. One must know whom he should obey. With regard to religion, we are wise (prudent) to obey God, though it should be kept in mind that in obeying God we are often obeying ourselves at the same time. This should not be surprising, since God's good for us and the good we rightly perceive for ourselves is the same good.

Command Performance

But the matter goes further than this. Obeying God is so important that He *commands* us to obey Him. The matter is not negotiable:

> I set before you this day a blessing and a curse: the bless-
> ing, if you obey the commandments of the LORD your
> God, which I command you this day, and the curse, if

you do not obey the commandments of the LORD your
God, but turn aside from the way which I command this
day, to go after other gods which you have not known
(Deut. 11:26-28).

God does not *invite* us to obey Him. Such a tepid disposition would suggest a less-than-fervent love. Disobeying
Him is not an option that He cordially extends to us. He
commands us to obey. Similarly, when Queen Elizabeth II
mailed personal announcements regarding the wedding of
her son, the Prince of Wales, to Lady Diana, she *commanded* her subjects to be present at the wedding. The
Queen *commands* obedience; she does not invite it. One
obeys the Queen. A *fortiori*, one obeys the Lord.

Mary, Our Model

In the Swahili version of the Hail Mary, the word
"Holy," as in "Holy Mary," is *mtakatifu*. Here, the Swahili
language offers us an interesting and valid insight into the
concept of Mary's holiness. *Taka* means "desire," while *tifu*
refers to "obedience." As a whole, the word *mtakatifu* means
"one who desires to be obedient." Mary is holy because she
is fully obedient to the will of God. She freely unites her
will with God's so that it not only affirms her own good, but
the good of all God's children as well. Mary, therefore, is
truly a universal mother.

While the secular mind has difficulty with the concept
of obedience, it has no difficulty in regarding loyalty as an
important virtue. Yet loyalty and obedience are very close
to each other. Loyalty requires a strong allegiance, if not
obedience, to a group. The loyal person must often make
sacrifices on an individual level for the good of the group
to which he belongs. Acts of disloyalty are more easily

viewed as betrayal and selfishness than acts of individual growth. Disloyalty to the Mafia is sometimes seen as less tolerable than disobedience to God; likewise, disloyalty to one's political party is less excusable than disobedience to one's spouse.

Nonetheless, obedience, as a virtue, is superior to the virtue of loyalty. It is more personal (rather than group directed) and, when it comes to obeying God, takes on a supernatural quality. In praying to God, one seeks trans-formation from unyielding resistance to obedience. Christ was obedient to death, death on the Cross (Phil. 2:8). He was obedient to His parents (Lk. 2:51) and advises us to be obedient as well: to Him, to His commandments, and to the truth.

True Freedom

It is most reasonable (prudent) to obey the person who loves you and knows the truth about your being. In this regard, a certain French philosopher speaks well when he writes, "Love makes obedience lighter than liberty." The virtue of obedience is not contrary to freedom, nor does it represent a master/slave or dominance/submission relation-ship. It both presupposes and anticipates freedom. Moreover, it establishes and perfects a relationship of love.

Obedience, therefore, is closely allied to *service*. Hence the expressions "your will is my command" and "it is a pleasure to serve you." The person who loves is happy to serve, eager to obey the needs and desires (legitimate ones, of course) of the beloved. Obedience allows a person to transcend the narrow confines of egotism and respond to the good of those he loves with alacrity, enthusiasm, and cheerfulness.

· GRATITUDE ·

In Luke 17:11-19, we read the story of the ten lepers. Jesus was traveling between Samaria and Galilee. As He entered a certain town (scholars believe it was Jenin, a pleasant little town seated on a hill in the midst of orchards and watercourses), ten lepers implored Him from an appropriate distance to have mercy on them. Jesus responded by instructing them to show themselves to the priests. This was not a cure but the promise of a cure. Lepers could be readmitted to society only after they had been certified by priests that they were completely clean. Obedient to the Master's instruction, the lepers made their way to the priests. En route, miraculous cures began to transpire. One of the ten, a Samaritan, returned to Jesus to express his gratitude. After prostrating himself before the feet of Jesus and offering copious thanks, the Samaritan heard Him say, to all who were present: "Were not ten cleansed? Where are the nine? Was no one found to return and give glory to God except this foreigner?" (Luke 17:17-18).

First Thanksgiving

This story makes it clear that gratitude pleases Jesus very much, while its absence brings Him sorrow. All ten showed humility, reverence, obedience, and faithfulness. We have neither the means nor the right to pass judgment on the nine who did not return to Jesus to express their gratitude. Perhaps they felt that their most urgent obligation was to present themselves before the priests. We do not know, though even postponing their expression of gratitude called forth their Savior's sorrowful expression.

The fact that Jesus did not cure all ten lepers immediately gave them the opportunity to decide whether or not they should return to Him directly and express their gratitude as soon as their cures took place. The delayed miracle allows the story to underscore the significance of gratitude and invites us to reflect on why Jesus prizes it so highly.

Count Our Blessings

Gratitude is a response to a gift. Because there is a wide range in the importance of gifts, there is, correspondingly, an equally wide range in levels of gratitude. For lesser gifts, such as giving someone the time of day, a simple expression of thanks is little more than a courtesy. But the large gifts— life itself, a miraculous cure, sacramental gifts—demand that gratitude include far more than a gesture of courtesy. God's generous presence in our lives lays claim to a form of gratitude that is never satisfied by the mere recitation of thanks, but requires us to express our gratitude in action. The kind of gratitude that God is hoping to find is one that includes a bond of friendship and a commitment to service.

God wants our full gratitude because He wants our continuing friendship, which enables Him to lavish us with additional gifts. We know how easy it is to be ungrateful, how a preoccupation with ourselves can cause us to forget our benefits as well as our benefactors. But in addition to that, ingratitude weakens our bonds with both God and neighbor. Saint Bernard has said: "Ingratitude is a searing wind which dries up the springs of pity, the dew of mercy, the streams of grace." Ingratitude leads to spiritual isolation. Therefore, gratitude, which is a triumph over selfishness and isolation, is most pleasing to God.

Timely Reminder

In 1863, during the American Civil War, President Abraham Lincoln was deeply concerned that America no longer seemed gratefully disposed to her Creator. In order to remind his fellow countrymen of their need to thank God and reestablish their friendship with Him, he proclaimed a national day of "humiliation, fasting, and prayer." On that day, Lincoln stated that although Americans had been the recipients of the choicest bounties of heaven, they had forgotten God:

> We have forgotten the gracious hand which preserved us in peace and multiplied and enriched and strengthened us, and we have vainly imagined, in the deceitfulness of our hearts, that all these blessings were produced by some superior wisdom and virtue of our own. Intoxicated with unbroken success, we have become too self-sufficient to feel the necessity of redeeming and preserving grace, too proud to pray to the God that made us.

Lincoln's understanding of the importance of gratitude was profound. He knew that a weakened relationship with God inevitably meant a weakened relationship with neighbor. The Civil War was ample testimony to that fact.

Better Than Santa

Gratitude is the memory of the heart, as someone has said. It is, therefore, an expression of love and abiding friendship. Gratitude is an expression that soon transforms itself into deed. Two ways we can express gratitude in our actions are through humility and restraint. As G.K. Chesterton has said, "We should thank God for beer and Burgundy by not drinking too much of them."

There can be no happiness without gratitude. We need to know whom to thank for the gift of life. But we also need to thank Him, and the proper form of thanks is to safeguard and cherish what we have been given. Humility and restraint are appropriate ways in which we can show how much we truly appreciate what has been given to us. To quote Chesterton once again:

> Children are grateful when Santa Claus puts in their stockings gifts of toys or sweets. Could I not be grateful to Santa Claus when he put in my stockings the gift of two miraculous legs?

· GENEROSITY I ·

It belongs to the nature of giving that a gift be given to another. Strictly speaking, one cannot give a gift to himself.

The highest gift we can give to another is the gift of ourselves. Giving ourselves in this way epitomizes the virtue of generosity. The perfect example of generosity is God the Creator. By means of His generosity, He generates man in His image. For Christians, God's gift of Himself through Christ represents the ultimate form of generosity, and serves as a model for all human generosity.

Because God creates—or generates—man in His image out of His own generosity, a dynamic impulse toward generosity is implanted in the depth of man's being. As a consequence, to live authentically means to give generously. Personality and generosity, therefore, are virtually synonymous. To live authentically is to give generously of oneself. The great Thomistic philosopher, Jacques Maritain, underscored this unification of personality with generosity when he wrote: "Do not heroes and saints impress us as men who have reached the heights of personality as well as generosity?"

Gotta Give

When a person is in touch with the depths of himself, he realizes that at the very center of his being, coincidental with his existence, is the impulse toward generosity. To be is to give; to be fulfilled is to have given generously. The very meaning of life is inseparable from generosity.

Everyone recognizes that generosity is more admirable than greed, and more beautiful, more original, more authentic, and more humane. The fact that greed is as common as it is indicates that human beings can be estranged from themselves while trying to live a life that is alien to them.

Since the time of Socrates, philosophers have been reiterating the essential importance of distinguishing between the order of *being* and *having*. Martin Buber wrote beautifully about the "I-Thou" relationship that cultivates our being, or our humanness, and the "I-It" relationship that allows us to have those things that allow us to live. Without "I-It" we cannot live, but without "I-Thou" we cannot be human. Things cannot humanize us, only generous love can.

Greed, the antithesis of generosity and the negation of personal being, enters the picture when our attachment to the things we can *have* displaces our awareness of our own *being*. But no amount of *having* can ever make up for a neglect of *being*. A form of frenzied addiction ensues when a person believes that if he could only have more of something, he would be able to quench his thirst. Unfortunately, the logic of greed is such that the appetite grows on what it feeds. This is the diabolical phenomenon that Shakespeare describes in *Macbeth* when he has Malcolm say: "[M]y more-having would be as a sauce to make me hunger more."

I Want More!

Nothing exceeds like excess! Greed becomes more avaricious the more it has. This paradoxical effect is connected with the fact that a person becomes increasingly frustrated the more he ignores his own fundamental capacity for generosity.

Literary characters such as King Midas, Silas Marner, Ebenezer Scrooge, and The Grinch Who Stole Christmas, are driven by greed in such a way that the more greedy they become, the less human they appear. The conversions of Midas, Marner, Scrooge, and the Grinch are, in effect, returns to humanity, and are met by readers with great jubilation. Generous people are not only more likeable than their greedy counterparts, but they appear to be more human, more real.

A wealthy man can easily become a displaced person, alienated from himself, if he takes his riches too seriously. Plato warned long ago that we should bequeath to our children not riches but reverence. Sigmund Freud explained that wealth never makes a man happy because it does not correspond to a basic human drive. None of us comes into the world with a desire to make money. The impulse to have does not originate in our being.

On the other hand, a poor man, who is in touch with the fundamental generosity of his existence, can be productive, happy, and at peace with himself. It is more blessed to give than to receive; but it is far more blessed to give than to take. In the final analysis, we cannot take with us what we have. Greed is an affliction of the dispossessed. Generosity is the plentitude of the self-possessed.

It Isn't Enough

Maurice Sendak has written a charming little book for children called *Higglety Pigglety Pop! or There Must Be More To Life*. In the story, the owners of Jennie the dog have given her everything. Yet she decides: "There must be more to life than having everything." She leaves home and loses all she has, but instead becomes the leading star of a theatrical production, to her great contentment. The point is made only too clear, even for ten-year-olds, that happiness depends not on *how much* we have, but on *who* we are. *Being* is more primary than *having*. And at the center of our being is the divinely implanted impulse to give and to be generous.

To the calculating mind, being generous seems to be costly. To the generous heart, being greedy seems incomprehensible. It is greed that impoverishes us, not generosity. True generosity, indeed, enriches us a hundredfold. There is a superabundance within each of us. Not to release it costs us who we are. Nothing, therefore, is more costly than greed; nothing is more rewarding than generosity.

· GENEROSITY II ·

Generosity inspires gratitude, and gratitude inspires generosity. God is generous to us and our generosity, as Saint Paul tells us, "gives proof of our gratitude towards God" (2 Cor. 9:11, Knox Bible). In gratitude we are human; in generosity we are divine: "You received without pay, give without pay" (Mt. 10:8).

The Virtue That Keeps Giving

An admirer of the great German composer, Johannes Brahms, left him one thousand pounds in his will. Upon learning about the bequest, Brahms was deeply moved. "It touches me most deeply and intimately," he wrote to a friend. "All exterior honors are nothing in comparison." Then, in the very next sentence, he informed his friend that since he did not need the money, he was "enjoying it in the most agreeable manner, by taking pleasure in its distribution."

Thus, the virtue that touched Brahms inspired replication of itself in the generosity that Brahms himself demonstrated. And one hopes that it stirred the same virtue among his beneficiaries. Generosity is the virtue that can go on mirroring itself until the end of time.

Logic or Madness?

What are the limits of generosity? Since virtue is rooted in love, this question is tantamount to asking, "What are the limits of love?"

Brad Barrows, age 37, of East Hartford, Connecticut, prayed that he would be able to do something exceptionally loving for someone. During prayer he felt a powerful call to donate a kidney. The call was so vivid and compelling that, in his judgment, "it sounded almost like a voice."

Barrows contacted the National Kidney Foundation and was told that he did not qualify as a donor because he was neither dead nor had a friend or loved one in need of a kidney. Undeterred, he got in touch with the Hartford Transplant Associates. There he found a sympathetic ear in its coordinator, Cathy Drouin. Nonetheless, she knew that the idea of donating an organ to a perfect stranger would be repugnant to the medical world and advised Barrows that, if he were determined to donate a kidney, he would first have to prove his sanity. The logic of generosity can easily resemble the delirium of madness. Or, as John Bunyan once said: "A man there was tho' some did count him mad, the more he cast away, the more he had."

Barrows did manage to get psychiatric clearance and was matched up with a suitable prospective recipient: José Spivey, age twelve, who was spending eleven hours a day on a home-dialysis machine. In addition, José had to leave his home in Cromwell, Connecticut, three times a week for three-hour sessions at Hartford Hospital.

Barrows has become José's Big Brother (Big Brother is an organization that connects boys who are lacking a father with male mentors). Their first meeting was carried off with aplomb. José explained to Barrows how he used his home-dialysis equipment. Barrows explained the meaning of "Love God" on the gold-plated cross he wears around his neck.

"Love God" required some explaining, for it is inscribed in Braille. Brad Barrows is blind, a fact that makes his generosity—together with its complete absence of any hint of resentment—all the more inspirational.

"I'll literally be your blood brother," Barrows, who is white, explains to José, who is black. "You can feel free to share anything. That's what Big Brothers are for."

It remains to be seen whether the kidney transplant will be successful. But even if it should fail, the failure would not dim the luster of Brad Barrows' generosity. And, while it is a level of generosity we might not be able to imitate, it is surely one that we can admire.

Gift of Light

Hope is often associated with light. One refers, for example, to the "light at the end of the tunnel." The fact that a blind man is offering a young boy hope—while the rest of the world watches—attests to the spiritual nature of light and how it can emerge from the most unlikely places.

Generosity begets gratitude, which begets generosity. But all the while, as the cycle continues, it sends out sparks of hope. Thank God for Brad Barrows and the hope he is sending out from his own darkness to a world that is so urgently in need of light.

Generosity
You are most generous,
Accepting my poor poetry
As ample payment for your smile,
Mere words as fitting tribute
For your bright, vivacious style;

My praise, then, sinks me deeper in your debt,
Far enough to still my pen, except
For one redeeming fact that warrants this encore:
Artful acclamation makes
Your soul shine all the more.

· HOPE I ·

Early in his pontificate, His Holiness the Pope earned the nickname, "His Polishness the Hope." Pope John Paul II has been a virtual embodiment of hope.

In his preface to the Holy Father's *Crossing the Threshold of Hope*, Vittorio Messori remarks that Pope John Paul II is so impatient in his apostolic zeal that he "wants to shout from the rooftops (today crowded with television antennae) that there is hope, that it has been confirmed, that it is offered to whoever wants to accept it."[1]

In *Tertio Millennio Adveniente*, published in the same year as *Crossing the Threshold of Hope*, the Pope speaks of the importance of hope in the context of crossing "the threshold of the new millennium" (no. 33). He indicates that these "crossings" imply a measure of difficulty as well as a need for purification.

Hope Springs Eternal

"Good" hope, to use Saint Paul's qualifying adjective (2 Thess. 2:16), must be distinguished from the many false hopes that surround us daily and are constant sources of temptation. We hope for wealth, beauty, fame, success, and a comfortable life. But these are largely vanities. They will not furnish us with what satisfies our deepest longing. They are transitory; we are immortal.

---

[1] Pope John Paul II, *Crossing the Threshold of Hope*, Vittorio Messori, ed. (New York: Alfred A. Knopf, 1994), viii.

The Holy Father reminds us that good hope—or true hope—directs us to our final goal which gives ultimate meaning and value to everything that is part of our lives. Therefore, as he goes on to say:

> Christians are called to prepare for the Great Jubilee of the beginning of the Third Millennium *by renewing their hope in the definitive coming of the Kingdom of God*, preparing for it daily in their hearts, in the Christian community to which they belong, in their particular social context, and in world history.[2]

Hope is about that which is ultimate—God—but it is not unrelated to the events that make up the substance of our lives. Indeed, hope transfigures them precisely because it relates them to their ultimate meaning. Hope is ultimate and immanent. But it is also essential, for no human being can endure its opposite—despair.

Highway to Hell

In his great poem, *The Divine Comedy*, Dante penned what may be his most celebrated line when he inscribed over the entranceway to hell these words: "All hope abandon, ye who enter here" ("*Lasciate ogni speranza, voi ch'entrate*"). The immediate meaning, that hell is a place of absolute finality where hope is no longer possible, is clear enough.

But there is a subtler and perhaps more important meaning that pertains not to the inhabitants of hell but to those whose final destinies have not yet been determined. This slightly veiled meaning informs people about how they can book passage to hell. For if hell is a place without hope, then by living without hope one is preparing for eternal

---

[2]*Tertio Millennio Adveniente*, no. 46, original emphasis.

tenancy in hell. When we live without hope, we take on the hopeless condition of hell, and at the same time make it our logical destiny. What we need, therefore, is an endless hope so that our lives do not come to a hopeless end.

The fact that hope is essential to man by no means makes it easy to acquire. The hope that Pope John Paul II is writing about in both *Crossing the Threshold of Hope* and *Tertio Millennio Adveniente* is something we must attain, secure, and purify through considerable difficulty.

Weathering the Storm

One of the stormiest, if not *the* stormiest, cape in the world is the Cape of Good Hope, located near the southern tip of Africa where the powerful currents of the Atlantic and Indian Oceans converge. When Portuguese navigator Bartholomeu Dias discovered this cape in 1488, he called it, fittingly, the "Cape of Storms." Later King John II of Portugal renamed it "Cape of Good Hope" in anticipation of finding a sea route to India. Vasco da Gama later proved the king right when he sailed around the cape and discovered the long-sought passage to India.

In this narrative, history and symbolism come together. The hope of finding a sea route to India was eventually fulfilled because hope had been kept alive. This is the historical fact. But added to this is the symbolism that the hope was a good hope inasmuch as it was forged in a climate of difficulty. The stormy cape provided the crucible in which hope was tested and purified so that it could emerge as "good hope." As Ralph Waldo Emerson once wrote: "Hope never spread her golden wings but in unfathomable seas."

Woody Allen once remarked that "marriage is the loss of hope." If he meant that marriage brings about the loss of vain and unprofitable illusion, he is correct. But disillusionment is not the same as the loss of hope. We often do not grasp real hope until its impostor has been dashed by disappointment. The disillusionment that often occurs within marriage is not the death of hope if through it the couple learns to accept the lack of perfection in each other and embraces the demands of true love.

"Hope does not disappoint" (Rom. 5:5)

Real hope is not crushed by disappointment. In fact, it is in difficulty that hope often is born. As G.K. Chesterton said:

> As long as matters are really hopeful, hope is a mere flattery or platitude; it is when everything is hopeless that hope begins to be a strength at all. Like all the Christian virtues, it is as unreasonable as it is indispensable.

Good hope, therefore, has the qualities of realism, courage, patience, and the willingness to embrace difficulties. By contrast, what we might describe as "easy hope" lacks these virtuous qualities and is merely a wish for better things that has the aura of vanity or fantasy.

Hope is both ultimate and immanent, essential and difficult, natural and supernatural. It may well be compared, as the Pontiff states, citing Saint Paul, with a mother in labor, for the mother, anticipating the birth of her child, incorporates all of these elements.[3] The whole world is groaning under the weight of vanity. It is yearning to give birth to everlasting life and to share in the glorification of the sons of God (cf. Rom. 8:19-21). As the Holy Father reminds us, ours is a time of great trial, but also of great hope.

---

[3] Cf., *ibid.*, no. 23.

· HOPE II ·

Red Green is one of Canada's most endearing comic characters. Though a consummate bungler, who is completely inept at anything he tries to do, he lives by the maxim, "If the ladies don't find you handsome, at least they should find you handy." His handyman philosophy is as simple as it is myopic: Anything that is broken can be fixed by the proper application of duct tape. Needless to say, duct tape is neither the way to a woman's heart nor a panacea for every technological breakdown. But comedy is rarely divorced from philosophy. The valid insight that underlies Red Green's humor is that things are breaking down all around us and we are not only ill-equipped to meet the challenge, but are too enamored by bogus remedies to recognize our own ineptitude. By contrast, Dr. Ruth Westheimer is a tragedian because she actually believes that condoms are a virtual panacea for all of society's sexual problems. If Red Green were to take himself seriously, he would be equally as dangerous.

Blind Despair

Like Pagliaccio, we often find ourselves laughing on the outside while crying on the inside. Or more relevant to our secular predicament, we preoccupy ourselves with entertainment while the world, through our neglect, goes to pieces. Søren Kierkegaard thought that this is the way the world will end:

It happened that a fire broke out backstage in a theater. The clown came out to inform the public. They thought it was just a jest and applauded. He repeated his warning, they shouted even louder. So I think the world will come to an end amid general applause from all the wits, who believe that it is a joke.

Secular man is naïve enough to believe that he'll be fine as long as he has a good job, a shrewd tax consultant, and a generous retirement package. Then something happens, something that is both unexpected and beyond the reach of his coterie of professional repairmen.

Marginal Existence

The German philosopher Karl Jaspers writes about *Grenzsituation*, when our existence is at a margin, such as during acute loneliness, bereavement, imprisonment, or exile. In situations of this nature, we are thrown into a world of anguish that presents problems that cannot be resolved by actuaries.

In his autobiography, *The Pillar of Fire*, Karl Stern describes his personal situation after he had fled Nazi Germany. He had left behind many friends and relatives, and faced a new and uncertain life in an unknown world. He saw himself as one who, having escaped shipwreck, was left to spend the night alone in a lifeboat. It was while he was in this mood of existential uncertainty, this "shuddering exposure to fear," as he termed it, that he first came into contact with the philosophy of Saint Thomas Aquinas. The Angelic Doctor's understanding of the virtue of hope was a revelation to him. Until that point, Stern regarded hope as something related to wish, rather than as a virtue. Now he was being introduced to a "lofty Christian anthropology" in which hope could be grasped not only as a supernatural virtue, but as an indispensable beacon of light in our journey through life.

Indeed, for Aquinas, life is a journey. Man is *homo viator*, a wayfarer, a pilgrim. He is not *homo comprehensor*, the being who comprehends or even plans his future. As *homo viator*, he avoids the extremes of despair and presumption. Despair results when hope seems impossible; presumption occurs when hope seems unnecessary. As pilgrims, we live by hope.

We have a nature whose intelligibility is discovered through reason. But our nature has a destiny that transcends reason. Thus, we need supernatural virtues, such as hope. Our anthropology is not complete until our nature is fused with our supernatural destiny.

Destined for Virtue

We begin with nature. And nature is rich with implication. Yet, if all we can discern exists on a purely natural plane, we inevitably become either comedians or tragedians, offering the world a simpleminded solution to the complexity of human existence.

Red Green's duct tape is the perfect image for the limitations of the secular mind. The only way to do justice to nature is to wed it to the realm of the supernatural. Divorced from its supernatural implications, the natural soon becomes the unnatural. At this point, we become either comedians or tragedians, but neither philosophers nor theologians.

G.K. Chesterton once remarked that he did not have the patience to be a philosophy teacher because he could not "suffer fools gladly." His remark was not a sign of arrogance, but a rather humorous observation that philosophy teachers, as a matter of course, blandly go about separating, for the benefit of the misguided neophyte, what is normal from what is ludicrous. "Cause" precedes, not supersedes, "effect"; the whole is greater than the part; a human being has free will, but a stone does not; and so on.

Reality Bytes

At the heart of Aquinas' philosophy is an axiom of similar obviosity: "The human intellect is measured by things so that man's thought is not true on its own account but is called true in virtue of its conformity with things."[1]

This statement is so incontestable that it has a certain aesthetic quality, similar to a beautiful prayer. Nonetheless, it needs to be restated. The inclination toward selfishness that arises from original sin can also poison one's philosophical outlook. The selfish person treats himself as more important than others, but the selfish philosophy virtually denies the existence of the other. Aquinas reminds us of two duties: (1) to acknowledge the existence of things other than ourselves; (2) to subordinate our mind to those things as a way of recognizing their truth. Philosophy begins with these elementary acts of justice toward the universe.

This axiom that Aquinas states, so simply and elegantly, has unlimited practical significance. Much of our frustration in life stems from assigning too much importance to our ego and too little to everything else. The premise that my ego will never be frustrated is not a realistic basis for hope. The ego has a place, but a rather small one in relation to everything else. The ego needs a long apprenticeship in the art of deference. Real hope is more concerned about finding one's place than getting one's way. To "stand in

---

[1] *Summa Theologiae*, IIa IIae, q. 9, art. 2.

authentic place," to borrow a phrase from Shakespeare, is to achieve one's destiny. But this accomplishment requires a great deal of honesty and humility.

To the question, "What can I do with philosophy?" Martin Heidegger once responded that the real point is "What can philosophy do with me?" We sometimes foolishly think that anything that brings us comfort is practical, and anything that reminds us of our obligations is not. Eyelids are practical, but not nearly as practical as the eyesight they protect.

· FORGIVENESS I ·

On the day after Christmas in 1996, the Canadian Broadcasting Company (CBC) did a television program from Toronto on the subject of "forgiveness." There were four panelists on the show; I was one of them. As might be expected, we disagreed on virtually every aspect of this extraordinary and indispensable virtue. But there was some agreement.

Half of the panel agreed that forgiveness is supernatural. But my lone ally on this point deserted me on the issue of whether a person can forgive himself. It seemed rather curious to me, however, that a person could hold that forgiveness is supernatural and that one can forgive himself. The implication here is that one is his own supernatural source for forgiving himself of his own sins. Can a person be both God and sinner, confessor and penitent at the same time? This notion seemed so strained to me that I thought it qualified as an excellent example of Orwellian "doublethink." Nonetheless, I was alone in believing that forgiveness is supernatural and that a person cannot, strictly speaking, forgive himself.

My thoughts flashed back to Paul Vitz's book, *Psychology as Religion: The Cult of Self-Worship*. It is not entirely unusual for certain forms of psychology to encourage people to worship themselves. "*You* are the Supreme being," Carl Frederick tells his readers in *est: Playing the Game the New Way*.

Easy Way Out

Forgiving oneself remains a trendy and popular distortion of forgiveness simply because it is attractive. And it is attractive because it is simple, swift, cheap, painless, and does not require us to face the social and interpersonal implications of our sins. We can be very easy on ourselves when we believe that our sins have no implications beyond ourselves.

The notion that we can forgive ourselves, on one hand, appears self-centered; on the other hand, it is contradictory. Does it make any sense to divide oneself into two parts—the part that forgives and the part that is forgiven—and proceed to be both confessor and penitent to oneself? Moreover, can the part that forgives forgive itself? Such a notion is obviously absurd. But we should not expect much sense or much unity from a CBC-TV show that goes out of its way to orchestrate conflict on a subject that is essentially supernatural. In fact, one panelist opined that the Catholic Church should get out of the forgiveness business and leave the matter to the judicial system.

Mark 2:1-12 relates a most wonderful and charming story about Christ's forgiving a paralytic. Four men had carried their friend on a stretcher-bed to Capernaum to meet their Master. But when they arrived at the house where Christ was preaching, the crowds that had arrived from many towns in Galilee and Judea made it impossible for them to enter. Undaunted, the four men removed part of the roof that sheltered Christ and lowered the paralytic through the opening they had created. Jesus was struck by the faith and audacity of these men. He forgave the sick man's sins and also cured him of his paralysis.

The association of forgiveness with a miraculous restoration to physical health helps us to deepen our understanding of the unity of the soul and body, as well as the supernatural quality of forgiveness. The fact that the road to forgiveness was extremely difficult reminds us that the penitent is better disposed to receive forgiveness if his journey to forgiveness is, if not an ordeal, at least a matter of some discomfort and struggle.

Nothing More Than Feelings?

There are psychological barriers to forgiveness. We tend to rationalize, project our guilt onto others, deny, repress, and displace. But there are external barriers to forgiveness as well. In the story of the paralytic, the barrier was the crowd. The paralytic's friends, however, were able to overcome this barrier. Yet in doing so, they encountered another type of barrier, one of a social or conventional nature—respect for the private property of another. In the contemporary world, this type of barrier may appear in the form of political correctness. The world of political correctness tells us that guilt is man-made, an "erroneous zone," something that can be injurious to our self-esteem, and so on. Such barriers can be very effective in discouraging people from going to Confession.

The notion of real guilt is not fashionable these days. To a certain extent, real guilt has been replaced by "guilt feelings," a Freudian concept that has little to do with a moral transgression. Political correctness, which is naïvely committed to protecting people from all discomfort and anything that could possibly be offensive, wants to deny that guilt has any real foundation. One provides a far greater service for people, however, by helping them to expiate their sins through Confession than to help them repress their sins under a blanket that is woven of political correctness. Psychoanalytic humanist Erich Fromm, who is not a Christian, points out in his book *The Sane Society* that, "All figures show that Protestant countries have a much higher suicide rate than Catholic countries" and suggests that one explanation for this is "the more adequate means to deal with a sense of guilt by the Catholic Church."

With the Help of My Friends

The Capernaum story beautifully draws our attention to the important role friends can play, spiritually, physically, and socially, in helping us to get to Confession. The image of four apparently robust men carrying the paralytic on a stretcher-bed for a considerable distance is a graphic image of the strong helping the weak. Commenting on this passage, Saint Ambrose exclaims, "How great is the Lord, who through the merits of some, forgives others!"

The love that the friends have for the paralytic plays an important role in the process of forgiveness. The paralytic himself displays the humility that is indispensable for true forgiveness. He allows himself to be carried in full view of the assembled crowd on his pallet. Here we find the most commonly understood form of forgiveness: the humble penitent seeking to be forgiven of his sins.

A less common, but more exalted, form of forgiveness takes place between the victim and the transgressor. In this case (Saint Maria Goretti comes to mind), the virtue of magnanimity is required. The humble person seeks forgiveness for his sins, but the magnanimous person is able to offer forgiveness to those who sin against him. Furthermore, it is especially magnanimous to forgive one's transgressors, even when they do not request to be forgiven. Christ forgave His executioners from the Cross, even though they offered no indication of being repentant.

This form of forgiveness, although exceedingly difficult, is most God-like. "Nothing makes us like unto God," wrote Saint John Chrysostom, "as being always ready to forgive."

The unreadiness to forgive those who harm us, on the other hand, creates formidable problems. The victim who does not forgive his assailants, in effect, binds their injustice to himself and in the process deprives himself of peace of heart. The consequence of refusing to forgive others, in this case, often results in a person becoming increasingly bitter.

Goes Both Ways

The Lord's Prayer reminds us that peace is a consequence of both forms of forgiveness. The words, "Forgive us our trespasses as we forgive those who trespass against us," indicate that requesting forgiveness should not be divorced from dispensing it. In fact, Christ tells us that God will not extend forgiveness to those who refuse to forgive others. "For if you forgive men their trespasses, your heavenly Father also will forgive you; but if you do not forgive men their trespasses, neither will your Father forgive your trespasses" (Mt. 6:14-15). God will be magnanimous to us as we are magnanimous to others. Surely the way of magnanimity and peace is superior to the way of pride and bitterness.

North American society attaches a great deal of importance to the individual, often at the expense of his social obligations. Too much emphasis on the individual inevitably means not enough emphasis on the community. This atmosphere of individualism is not conducive to a spirit of forgiveness. Forgiveness is concerned with repairing relationships, between man and God, man and neighbor. Individualism withdraws from relationships and centers on the individual himself. Therefore, in a climate of individualism, there is a marked tendency for people either to refrain from forgiveness altogether or to opt for "forgiving" themselves.

The decline in the popularity of the confessional over the past few decades is no doubt intertwined with a decline in communal spirit and neighborly love. Forgiveness, along with all other true virtues, is founded on love. The virtue of forgiveness, however, requires a host of other virtues, including humility, magnanimity, clemency, mercy, justice, patience, courage, and hope. Yet, exalted as forgiveness is, it remains indispensable for everyday communal life. We simply must forgive our neighbor if we hope to be forgiven ourselves. This is the great paradox of forgiveness, that the highest and the lowest, the most supreme and the most humble, stand together. But this is also the essential feature of Christ, that He is God, and at the same time a human being who walks with us and dwells in our hearts.

· FORGIVENESS II ·

The exalted nature of forgiveness is attested to by the fact that it presupposes a number of other virtues. Consider three virtues in particular: justice, clemency, and mercy. Justice has the nature of an equation: borrowing ten dollars requires returning ten dollars. When justice is violated, punishment or restitution of some kind is required. Herein is the timeless significance of bringing the scales of justice back into balance. Injustice demands a counterbalancing repayment. Clemency goes beyond justice, to some extent ignoring the need for precise balancing, and reduces the payment. Clemency, for example, may be used to reduce a sixty-day sentence to fifteen days. Mercy goes beyond both justice and clemency to wipe away the need for punishment. It does not turn a blind eye to the offense committed, but it does pardon the offender. Forgiveness goes beyond these three virtues, but without negating any of them. In fact, justice, clemency, and mercy provide the very foundation that allows forgiveness to be a possibility. Forgiveness goes beyond mercy and treats the offense as if it never happened. It wipes the slate clean, as it were, and gives the transgressor a fresh start.

On the part of the person forgiven, the virtues of humility, sincerity, and hope are presupposed. In this way, forgiveness represents a truly exalted virtue because of the foundational virtues it presupposes in both the forgiver and the one forgiven.

Humanly Possible?

So exalted is forgiveness that it has long been described as supernatural. "To err is human, but to forgive is divine." Or, to modify this timeless maxim slightly, "To err is human, but to forgive is superhuman." By contrast, systems of justice are incapable of dispensing forgiveness. A sign posted in a Los Angeles police station brings this point home both accurately and humorously: "To err is human, to forgive is against departmental policy."

Systems that are human are not only incapable of forgiving, but are often vehemently opposed to it. A few years ago a successful businessman died whose name happens to be well-known to enthusiasts of baseball trivia. National circulation newspapers that carried his obituary began, not in the customary manner by mentioning his accomplishments or enumerating the members of his immediate family, but in the following manner: "Fred Snodgrass, whose muff of a fly ball cost the New York Giants the 1912 World Series. . . ." Society remembers Fred Snodgrass, along with "Wrong Way" Corrigan and a populous class of similar individuals, solely in terms of a single, inexcusable, though often trivial, misadventure.

In order to be in a position to appreciate the reasonableness of forgiveness (and the accompanying horror of condemnation), one must stand on a platform built on its foundational virtues. It is comparable to a father lifting up his child so that the lad can see over the heads of the people in front of him and see the parade.

No Islands

The secular world has its penitentiaries, just as hockey has its penalty boxes and baseball score cards have their error columns. The kind of forgiveness the world usually offers is of a bogus variety—that of forgiving yourself. This concept of self-forgiveness is, in part, the consequence of modern secular psychology that has inflated the importance of the individual as an individual. Popular self-help books such as *How to Be Your Own Best Friend*, *Winning Through Intimidation*, *How to Get Divorced from Mom and Dad*, and others, create the impression that the individual is an island universe unto itself.

But forgiving oneself implies a radical form of personal disunity. Can one divide oneself into two parts: the part that bestows forgiveness and the part that receives forgiveness? And how would the former part receive forgiveness or rise above the latter part to presuppose that it can dispense forgiveness? And along what lines (fault lines?) of the personality can such a division be made?

Forgiveness, of its essence, concerns not individuals as such, but relationships. Forgiveness repairs a damaged relationship between man and God, as well as between man and neighbor. The two great commandments—to love God and to love neighbor—reiterated in the Lord's Prayer, underscore this meaning of forgiveness.

Exalted and Mundane

In Peter Shaffer's play, *Amadeus*, a demented Antonio Salieri, now an inmate of an insane asylum, rolls through the hallways in his wheelchair dispensing "forgiveness" to his fellow inmates for the "sin" of mediocrity. The Salieri character went mad precisely because he could not succeed, despite trying with all the power he could muster to forgive himself for not being the equal, as a composer, to Mozart.

An individual cannot forgive himself, no more than soap can clean itself. Humility is the virtue we need to be ourselves. Forgiveness is the virtue we need in order to repair our relationships with others.

In the absence of forgiveness (the presence of unrepaired relationships), the field is wide open for the unchecked spread of deadly vices. This is the theme of Friedrich Dürrenmatt's most enduring play, *Der Besuch der alten Dame* (*The Visit of the Old Woman*). In the play, first staged in 1956, Claire Zachanassian, now a very wealthy woman, returns to the town that unjustly condemned her and drove her out forty-five years earlier. Her unforgiving attitude hardens into hatred for all the townsfolk. Drawing on a huge amount of inheritance money, she exploits the greed of the people of Güllen, seduces them into murdering her principal defamer, and leaves town with the diabolical satisfaction that the collective guilt of the people will plague them for many years to come.

The fundamental paradox of forgiveness is that, although it is supernatural and presupposes many foundational virtues, it is also elementary and necessary in order for people to get along with each other on a day-to-day basis. Forgiveness is both exalted and mundane. This paradox may seem easier to grasp when one realizes that God, exalted as He is, remains with us to guide us in our relationships with Him and our neighbors every step of the way.

· ENDURANCE ·

She came into the world, according to her father, "kicking valiantly and crying obstreperously." Perhaps she had some premonition of the immense suffering she was destined to endure throughout the course of her life. Her father, on the other hand, no doubt regarded her protests with loving amusement. In retrospect, who can say which of the two displayed more wisdom on that momentous occasion?

We do know that on May 20, 1851, Rose Hawthorne, or "Rosebud" as her father, the celebrated novelist and short-story writer Nathaniel Hawthorne, affectionately called her, was born into an exceptionally happy and loving home. And Nathaniel's love for his daughter was fully reciprocated. Rose, who possessed no small literary gift of her own, once wrote, while reflecting on her stay in Rome as a youngster: "To play a simple game of stones on one of the gray benches in the late afternoon sunshine, with him for courteous opponent, was to feel my eyes, hands, all my being, glow with the fullest human happiness."

During that stay in the "Eternal City," the Hawthorne family was exposed, and most favorably so, to Catholicism. Seeds were planted that were to bear fruit in the lives of the children, especially Rose, many years later. An amusing incident occurred when little Rose left her mother one day and went dashing about in the Vatican Gardens. She suddenly bumped into someone who was walking toward her. It was none other than the Holy Father himself, the saintly Pio Nono (Pope Pius IX). He was most gracious and placed his hand on her tumbled red curls and gave her his blessing. An excited Rose could talk of nothing else all the way home.

Heart of Sorrow

The first great sorrow entered Rose's life when her father died suddenly on the day before her thirteenth birthday. Seven years later, her mother died of pneumonia. In the autumn of that same year, 1871, Rose married George Lathrop, a talented and aspiring writer. Tragedy, however, soon struck again. The only child they would ever have, Francie, died of diphtheria at the tender age of five. It was a crushing blow for the Lathrops, and they sought many avenues of diversion in order to fill the void left by their child's passing.

The Lathrops embarked on a spiritual journey. They commenced a serious study of Catholicism and began attending Mass with Catholic friends. They were received into the Catholic Church in 1891. Another sorrow, however, was on the horizon. Two years later, husband and wife were separated. It was said that their differences in temperament had finally won out. According to a friend, they were the original two of whom it was said that they could not live together nor apart. This alleged difference in temperament, however, was probably not as corrosive of their marriage as the "illness" which Rose tried her best to keep hidden from the world. George's chronic drinking problem took its toll on him. In 1898, at the age of forty-six, he died in the hospital of cirrhosis of the liver.

If George sought the comfort of alcohol to assuage his sorrow or to help fill the void created by the loss of his only child, Rose responded by charging straight into the very heart of sorrow. As she once confided to a friend, "A married woman, loving children as I do and bereft of them, must, it seems to me, fill the void in her life with works of charity." What would her beloved father have had her do? Among the first words she remembered him ever saying to her was, "Home duties are not so necessary or loving as duty toward the homeless."

Cancer patients in particular would become the object of her solicitude, especially those dying of incurable cancer. Her good friend Emma Lazarus, who labored for Russia's persecuted Jews, and who wrote the poetic inscription that is found on the base of the Statue of Liberty in New York City, had died of cancer. This tragic and untimely event had a strong influence on how Rose would spend the next thirty years of her life.

Resolute in Suffering

Rose Hawthorne Lathrop had endured a wave of terrible sufferings. Rather than indulge even in a hint of self-pity or any other crippling emotion that would deflect her commitment to performing works of charity, she endured her sufferings and remained steadfast. Aquinas states that endurance (*sustinere*) is "an action of the soul cleaving most resolutely [*fortissime*] to good."[1] He writes about how it is much more difficult to endure than to attack, to bear suffering than to become enraged about it.

---

[1] *Summa Theologiae*, IIa IIae, q. 123, art. 6.

She took a three-month course at the New York Cancer Hospital. When the course was over, she began the work that would occupy the remaining thirty years of her life. She began caring for those who were dying of incurable cancer and had no compassionate refuge to shelter them through their final days. She began by visiting cancer patients in their homes. She then proceeded to take patients into her own home, but soon needed to move into larger quarters. Using her literary talents, she was able to solicit donations and recruit personal assistance by writing newspaper articles. She also published a small magazine to publicize her work which she called *Christ's Poor*. Money came in, and volunteers, including medical personnel, offered their services. Rose's apostolate was growing.

On September 14, 1899, Rose Hawthorne became Sister Mary Alphonsa. She and her close friend, Alice Huber, founded the Servants of Relief for Incurable Cancer (now known as the Hawthorne Sisters). As members of this newly established branch of the Dominican Order, they offered free care to indigent sufferers of incurable cancer. Their work became more widely known and attracted support from far and wide. Novelist Mark Twain became one of their steadiest and most generous benefactors. In a personal letter to Mother Alphonsa, the great humanist assured her that her work would be permanent and would continue to prosper for, as he wrote, it "is banked where it cannot fail until pity fail in the hearts of men. And that will never be."

In time, seven hospitals were built. These hospitals stand today and continue to offer loving care at no cost to incurable cancer patients who have no money of their own.

Loving Quarters

Sister Alphonsa strove to put her patients "in such a condition that if Our Lord knocked at the door I should not be ashamed to show what I have done." One day, not God, but the renowned psychiatrist and expert on death and dying, Elisabeth Kübler-Ross, knocked on the door of the Rose Hawthorne Lathrop Home in Fall River, Massachusetts. She was so favorably impressed that she cited it in one of her books on death and dying as an ideal environment for the care of the terminally ill.

After Mother Alphonsa died, shortly before her seventy-fifth birthday, several pages of jottings were found among her effects that attested to her complete acceptance of God's will: "I will obey God anywhere, at any time, with courage. I will see all things through the presence of God, thus freeing myself of personality and forgetting my existence." She exquisitely personified the essential paradox of Christianity that by doing God's will through imitating Christ, we most perfectly realize ourselves.

Mother Alphonsa was humanized through her suffering. Moreover, she used it to build a bridge uniting her not only with others who were suffering, but with Christ crucified. But in the process, she found herself through losing herself, preserved her soul from the void of despair, and gave it life in the fullest sense. Despite her self-effacement, Rose Hawthorne (Mother Alphonsa) achieved an unmistakably beautiful personal identity. And the more she deferred to God, the larger she grew in stature. Her sorrow, indeed, built bridges, but bridges with two-way traffic, leading to others and from others back to her loving heart. She not only endured through terrible suffering, she prevailed, and we can all be richer for her moving example. In her own words:

Sorrow, my friend,
when shall you come again,
When shall you come again?
The wind is slow, and the bent willows send
Their silvery motions wearily down the plain.
The bird is dead
That sang this morning
through the summer rain.

Sorrow, my friend,
I owe my soul to you,
And if my life with any glory end
Of tenderness for others, and the words are true
Said, honoring, when I'm dead,
Sorrow, to you the mellow praise,
the funeral wreath are due.[2]

---

[2] As reproduced in Katherine Burton, *Sorrow Built a Bridge* (New York: Longmans, Green and Co., 1937).

· FORBEARANCE ·

Shortly after the third birthday of her first-born, Mabel and her two boys left South Africa for England. Her husband, who was unable to vacate his banking post at the time, was to join her as soon as the opportunity arose. The opportunity never did arise. While still confined to South Africa and five thousand miles away from his family, he died as a result of a severe hemorrhage.

Her husband's untimely demise left Mabel nearly destitute. She found inexpensive lodging for herself and her two boys in a suburb of Birmingham. Not able to afford tuition fees, she decided to teach her sons at home. She proved to be a more than adequate home school teacher.

Mother's Sacrifice

Four years after her husband's death, Mabel, together with her sister, May, were received into the Catholic Church. Immediately, the wrath of their family descended upon them. Mabel's Methodist father was outraged, while May's Anglican husband forbade his wife from ever entering a Catholic church. Reluctantly, May felt obliged to obey, leaving her sister to endure the consequences of her conversion alone. And the consequences were considerable, both in terms of emotional stress as well as financial hardship. Nonetheless, nothing could shake Mabel's faith in her new religion. Indeed, she began giving Catholic instructions to her sons. Her eldest thus became a child convert at the tender age of eight.

A few years later, the family's deteriorating financial situation obliged them to find cheaper quarters. They moved to a house that was little better than a slum. The only consolation of their new abode was its proximity to the Birmingham Oratory, a large church established by Cardinal John Henry Newman more than fifty years earlier.

It was not long after Mabel occupied her new home that her health began to deteriorate. She was diagnosed with diabetes. When her eldest was but twelve, Mabel passed away. She had lived for thirty-four trouble-filled years. Yet she bore her hardships with great faith and without any apparent traces of acrimony.

Her older son would one day, in a letter to his own son, say of his mother:

> I witnessed (half-comprehending) the heroic sufferings and early death in extreme poverty of my mother who brought me into the Catholic Church; and received the astonishing charity of Francis Morgan.[1]

In her will, Mabel had appointed Father Morgan as the guardian of her two sons. Over the course of the following years, he proved to be a loving father figure and a generous provider.

Enduring Example

Forbearance is patient endurance under provocation and in the face of persistent difficulties. But it is also the capacity to suffer outrageous fortune with little or no complaint. Mabel, outcast and destitute as she was, remained a

---

[1] Humphrey Carpenter, *The Letters of J.R.R. Tolkien* (Boston: Houghton Mifflin Co., 1981), 340.

model of forbearance for her two sons. Nine years after her death, her first-born expressed his indebtedness to her in the following words:

> My own dear mother was a martyr indeed, and it was not to everybody that God grants so easy a way to His great gifts as he did to Hilary and myself, giving us a mother who killed herself with labor and trouble to ensure us keeping the faith.[2]

Providence has a mysterious way of bringing beauty out of ruins, splendor out of apparent hopelessness. The eldest son never lost his faith. His marriage, which lasted fifty-five years until his wife passed away, bore four children, of whom the first-born was ordained a Catholic priest.

The first of Mabel's two sons is better known to us as a writer. He is J.R.R. Tolkien, who, according to several polls, is not only the author of the twentieth century's greatest book—*The Lord of the Rings*—but is the century's greatest author. His books have sold more than fifty million copies worldwide, and there are no signs of his popularity abating.

Lord of the Rings

Tolkien's success as a writer is unimaginable apart from his formation as a Catholic. And his formation is inconceivable apart from the faith and forbearance of his mother. Tolkien's stories are magical and mystical, using what we can imagine to draw us closer to the primary reality that we long for but cannot imagine. Perhaps the greatest story concerning Tolkien is connected with the hidden mother who

---

[2] Humphrey Carpenter, *J.R.R. Tolkein: Autobiography* (London: George Allen and Unwin, 1977), 39.

is the invisible source and shaper of her elder son's prolific success. She is the still point of his moving world, the anonymity that has made his name a household word. She is truly the mother of the lord of *The Lord of the Rings*.

· PRUDENCE ·

Rolf Hochhuth's play, *The Deputy*, had its world premiere in Berlin in the year 1963. The "Deputy" is Pope Pius XII, the "Deputy" or Vicar of Christ. The play was soon translated into English and imported to Broadway in New York City. The playwright contends that Pope Pius XII, when he was the Sovereign Pontiff of the Catholic Church, might have prevented deportations and the mass murder of so many Jewish people had he spoken out against the Nazi extermination camps. His alleged "silence," according to Hochhuth, was criminal, inhuman, and cowardly.

The storm of controversy *The Deputy* generated and continues to generate is almost certainly the largest furor ever raised by a play in the history of drama. Hochhuth himself, an instant celebrity at the age of thirty-one, added to the storm's intensity when he came to the United States in 1964 accompanied by an unusual amount of media coverage, together with a great outpouring of emotion.

In reviewing the play in 1964, *The New York Times* stated that its "facts may be in dispute; the history imperfect; the indictment too severe." The Jesuit magazine *America* condemned the play as "an atrocious calumny against the memory of a good and courageous world leader occupying the Chair of Peter during one of the great crises of humanity." Cardinal Francis Spellman called the play "an outrageous desecration of the honor of a great and good man, and an affront to those who know his record as a humanitarian, who love him and revere his memory."

Careful Action

In response to the play's contention that the Pontiff was criminally responsible for the death of countless Jews, Jewish historian Pinchus Lapide set to work researching the matter. The result was his book, *Three Popes and the Jews*, in which he defended Pope Pius XII. According to Lapide, seven to eight hundred thousand Jewish survivors of the Nazi Holocaust owe their lives to the Pontiff's leadership.

The Pope may have, at times, been restrained (not "silent"), but he was not inactive. He was certainly prudent. In order to be effective in assisting the Jews, he often had to act surreptitiously. Had he been too outspoken, he most likely would have invited swift and severe retaliation from both the Fascists in Italy and the Nazis in Germany. On January 24, 1943, Nazi Foreign Minister Joachim von Ribbentrop instructed Germany's ambassador to the Holy See to advise the Pope that if he spoke out against the Third Reich, "Germany does not lack the physical means of retaliation." When Hochhuth was asked in an interview whether the Pope should have protested publicly, granted that his vocal opposition would have prompted retaliation, his answer was categorical: "Absolutely." Hocchuth had little affection for prudence.

Severe Retaliation

In April of 1942, the Catholic bishops of Holland published a letter that was read in every Catholic Church in that country. The letter denounced "the unmerciful and unjust treatment meted out to Jews by those in power in our country." The retaliation was swift and severe. The Nazis rounded up every Catholic religious they could find who had as much as a drop of Jewish blood. They deported some three hundred victims to Auschwitz where they put them to death in gas chambers. Among these victims was the Carmelite nun, philosopher, and mystic, Saint Edith Stein. The heroism of the Dutch bishops exacted a terrible price. In addition to the Catholics, the Nazis slaughtered 110,000 or 79 percent of Holland's Jewish population, the highest percentage in any Nazi-occupied nation in Western Europe.

Concerning the persecution of the Jews, Pope Pius XII said to Archbishop Giovanni Battista (later Pope Paul VI), "We would like to utter words of fire against such actions; and the only thing restraining us from speaking is the fear of making the plight of the victims worse."

In *The Pope and the Holocaust*, researchers John Rader and Kateryna Fedoryka provide evidence that Hitler had targeted both Popes Pius XI and Pius XII because of their pro-humanity efforts, which included stern repudiations of anti-Semitism. It was only too clear that the Pope could be most helpful if he remained alive and acted covertly. It is now well-known how nearly every Catholic convent in Europe was hiding Jews, and that the Vatican was instrumental in forging thousands of documents, especially in Southern France, to facilitate their emigration. The Pope was involved in the systematic work done by nuncios throughout Nazi-occupied Europe of enlightening the heads of governments in Catholic countries about the true and murderous meaning of the word "resettlement."

Gracious Appreciation

The Jewish community has not been silent about what Pope Pius XII did for his persecuted brethren. In October of 1945, the World Jewish Congress made a financial gift to the Vatican in recognition of the work the Holy See performed in rescuing Jews from Fascist and Nazi persecutions.

Dr. Israel Goldstein of the same World Jewish Congress said, on the occasion of Pope Pius XII's death:

> The Jewish community told me of their deep appreciation of the policy which had been set by the Pontiff for the Vatican during the period of the Nazi-Fascist regime to give shelter and protection to the Jews, whenever possible.

On the same occasion, Golda Meir cabled her condolences to the Vatican:

> When fearful martyrdom came to our people in the decade of Nazi terror, the voice of the Pope was raised for the victims. The life of our times was enriched by a voice speaking out on the great moral truths.

In February of 1945, the Chief Rabbi of Rome, Israel Zolli, and his wife, Emma Majonica, were baptized into the Catholic Church. Zolli took the name "Eugenio," Pope Pius XII's Christian name.

Pope Pius XII acted prudently. Prudence is a virtue closely allied with wisdom. It is usually best appreciated in its results rather than in its execution. For this reason, an observer may not recognize the prudence of a wise man at the moment he is acting prudently. But history offers us 20/20 hindsight. And history has shown that Pope Pius XII acted prudently. It also attests that he acted not only courageously, but also heroically.

· THANKFULNESS ·

The word *thank* is derived from the Old English *thanc*, meaning *thought*. *Thank*, therefore, is related to *think*. This is most fitting since there must be some thought before one can offer proper thanks. Giving thanks is the fruit of a thoughtful (and grateful) heart. Gratitude is the disposition; thanksgiving is its natural expression. Thankfulness, because it brings the mind and heart together, is an articulation of the whole person. Moreover, it disposes the person to express his thanks in sundry other virtuous ways, through generosity, patience, fidelity, and so on. Perhaps this helps us to understand why Cicero held that "a thankful heart is not only the greatest virtue, but the parent of all other virtues."

Godly Thought

Descartes, author of the most celebrated phrase in all of modern philosophy, stopped at thinking. Who knows how different the course of modern philosophy might have been had he proceeded from "I think, therefore I am," to declare, "I thank, therefore we are"? How much richer, the humble prayer of Shakespeare's *Henry VI*: "O Lord, that lends me life, lend me a heart replete with thankfulness."

To the Italian mind, the natural intimacy between God's grace and our thanks seems evident. *Grazia* is grace or favor, whereas *grazie* is thanks. For the Italian Christian, it is easy to understand how the expression *nell'anno di grazia* (in the Year of Our Lord) should give rise to its human echo, *nell'anno di grazie* (in the Year of Our Thanks). We give thanks for God's grace with graceful, or grateful, thanks of our own. *Grazie*, therefore, is the appropriate response to *grazia*.

Thanks, along with anything else that is so fundamental and obligatory, is all too easily dulled and degraded by endless repetition. "Thanks" is commonly said thoughtlessly, often barely above a whisper. "Thanks a lot," takes on a cynical cast. And "thanks for nothing," especially in an angry tone, is a searing insult.

Mission (Almost) Impossible

Christians are commanded to make sure that their thanks are heartfelt. But more than that, they are commanded to give thanks for *everything*. "[G]ive thanks in all circumstances;" Saint Paul writes, "for this is the will of God in Christ Jesus for you" (1 Thess. 5:18). It is easy to be thankful for good things, but to be thankful for difficulties— rejection, sickness, death, and so forth—at first glance seems to be absurd.

But Christian commandments are like this. They demand the seemingly implausible. Scripture enjoins us to love our enemies, do good to those who harm us, pray for those who persecute and calumniate us (Mt. 5:44). They obligate us to forgive, daily, those who trespass against us (Mk. 11:25). Mark Twain exquisitely captured both the beauty and difficulty of this demanding quality of Christian forgiveness when he said, "Forgiveness is the fragrance the violet sheds on the heel that crushed it." It is not that Christianity is indiscriminate, but that it is omnivorous! Virtues should be directed to all people, and at all times.

Christian thankfulness, which is to say, supernatural thankfulness, is inseparable from the theological virtues of faith, hope, and love. When David proclaims, "[G]ive thanks to the Lord, for he is good, for his steadfast love endures for ever" (Ps. 136:1), he is inviting us to have faith in God, to hope for good things, and to maintain our love for Him. True thankfulness is webbed to a multitude of virtues.

Piece of Mind

One of the most often repeated and widely honored spiritual phrases of the twentieth century dealing with thankfulness—or any other subject, for that matter—belongs to Dag Hammarskjöld, the former secretary general of the United Nations. The fact that it comes from a secular, political leader conferred upon it a certain added credibility: "For all that has been—Thanks! To all that shall be—Yes!"

Hammarskjöld understood that there could be no peace without an all-encompassing perspective within which one can offer thanks for tribulations. In this regard Hammarskjöld, who once likened his office to that of being a "Secular Pope," was in full accord with the thought of Blessed John of Avila: "One act of thanksgiving, when things go wrong with us, is worth a thousand thanks when things are agreeable to our inclinations." When we are smitten with tests and trials, a spirit of thanksgiving can be a most soothing antiseptic. We cannot be at peace at all times if we do not preserve an attitude of thankfulness at all times. It is a simple and natural thing to thank God for sending us the gifts we like; it is a virtuous and supernatural thing to thank Him for those gifts we do not like. God is glorified more perfectly by our thanks than by our groans.

In addition, thankfulness should be spontaneous and generous. Because we are creatures of a generous God, we should always be disposed to worship Him with thanks. Henry Ward Beecher could not have expressed this senti-ment more beautifully:

> As flowers carry dew drops, trembling on the edges of the petals, and ready to fall at the first waft of the wind or brush of bird, so the heart should carry its beaded words of thanksgiving.

EVERYBODY YOU'D EXPECT TO ENDORSE THIS BOOK HELPED TO WRITE IT.

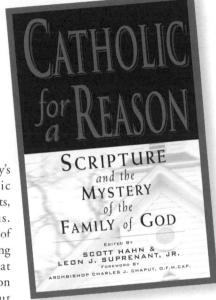

Imagine today's top Catholic authors, apologists, and theologians. Now imagine 12 of them collaborating on a book that answers common questions about and challenges to the teachings and doctrines of the Catholic Church. Imagine no more, it's a reality. (How's that for an endorsement?)

Catholic for a Reason, edited by Dr. Scott Hahn and Leon J. Suprenant, with the foreword by Archbishop Charles J. Chaput (yes, we're name-dropping), will help Catholics and non-Catholics alike develop a better understanding of the Church. Each chapter goes to the heart of its topic, presenting the teachings of the Church in a clear, concise and insightful way. The teachings on Mary, the Eucharist, Baptism, and Purgatory are explained in light of the relationship of God the Father to us.

Catholic for a Reason, published by Emmaus Road Publishing, Inc., is bound to become an apologetics classic. Call (800) 398-5470 to order your copy today. Retail price $15.95 + $3.00 s/h.

EMMAUS ROAD PUBLISHING

Emmaus Road Publishing
827 North Fourth Street, Steubenville, OH 43952
(800) 398-5470 • Fax: (740) 283-4011

www.emmausroad.org

Servants
of the Gospel

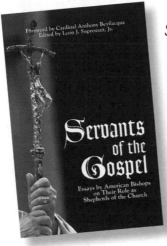

Servants of the Gospel is a collection of essays by American bishops on the bishop's role in the Church today. Authors such as Archbishop Charles J. Chaput of Denver and Cardinal Francis George of Chicago examine the unique and challenging task of the apostles' successors. This timely work is designed to foster lay collaboration with bishops as the Church continues Christ's mission into the third Christian millennium.

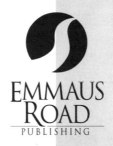